PRAISE FOR
THE KI...

PRAISES
FOR THE
KING OF KINGS

∽∾∽∾∽∾∽∾∽∾

WALTER J. CHANTRY

THE BANNER OF TRUTH TRUST

THE BANNER OF TRUTH TRUST
3 Murrayfield Road, Edinburgh EH12 6EL
PO Box 621, Carlisle, Pennsylvania 17013, USA

★

© *Walter J. Chantry 1991*
First published 1991
ISBN 0 85151 587 8

★

Typeset at the Spartan Press Ltd,
Lymington, Hants
Printed and bound in Great Britain by
BPCC Hazell Books
Aylesbury, Bucks, England
Member of BPCC Ltd.

Contents

TO HIM WHO LOVES US AND HAS FREED US FROM
OUR SINS BY HIS BLOOD, AND HAS MADE US TO BE
A KINGDOM AND PRIESTS TO SERVE HIS GOD AND
FATHER — TO HIM BE GLORY AND POWER FOR-
EVER AND EVER! AMEN.

Revelation 1:5–6

Introduction

'To you who believe, he (Jesus Christ, the Son of God) is precious' (*1 Peter 2:7*). Faith and love are twin graces. When trust in Jesus is born within a soul, so too is a holy affection toward the Saviour brought to birth. Every genuine believer cherishes and adores the Lord Jesus.

Those who are in love enjoy thinking about and talking about their dearly beloved. Better yet, the amorous heart longs to be in the presence of the one who is endeared. The theme of these meditations is the Delight of every Christian's heart – Jesus, the Lord. He is precious in the sight of God the Father, whose testimony is, 'This is my Son, whom I love; with him I am well pleased' (*Matthew 3:17*). Our spirits echo this sentiment. He is our Lord, whom we love; we are entirely pleased with him.

Samuel Rutherford once exclaimed, 'Black sun, black moon, black stars, but, O bright, infinitely bright Lord Jesus!' Isaiah predicted the coming of our blessed Redeemer with these words, 'The glory of the Lord will be revealed, and all mankind together will see it' (*Isaiah 40:5*). 'The Son is the radiance of God's glory' (*Hebrews 1:3*). All of the beauty, loveliness and dignity of the infinite God that can be revealed to the creature man shines from the face of Christ. The person of Jesus Christ constitutes the perfect representation of God. He is the fullest self-manifestation of divine glory. 'In these last days God has spoken to us in his Son' (*Hebrews 1:2*). We would see more of Jesus! If only God's Spirit would open these psalms about the Messiah to our hearts as we ponder them, we will be satisfied.

As we in this modern age long to catch a fresh glimpse of our beloved Lord, we must recognize that many ancients shared our love for him. They too saw his glory, even thousands of years before his birth. Jesus himself taught that 'Abraham rejoiced at the thought of seeing my day; he saw it and was glad' (*John 8:56*). If you contemplate the psalms, you will realize that David, too, saw Jesus' day quite clearly indeed, and seeing, his gladness rose to thrilling heights.

These ancient believers did not have the benefit of all the objective revelation we possess. They were not with Christ when he came in the flesh. They did not have the finished, written Word of God, the New Testament Scriptures containing the testimony of those whose eyes saw, whose ears heard and whose hands touched the Word of life (*1 John 1:1*). So many captivating details of Jesus' person and work were unavailable to them. But what objective revelations of the coming Messiah they did possess were savoured by hearts eager to know him better, joyful at the prospect of beholding him whom their souls loved. Aided by the Holy Spirit of illumination, they had a clear knowledge of the glory of Christ, and their hearts burned within them with joyful recognition of him.

Perhaps many Christians experience so little of the joy of the Lord simply because little time is given exclusively to quiet meditation on the glories of our beautiful Saviour. It is tragic when any believer allows pressures and multiple activities to rob him of time alone with his Lord. For it is in the unhurried secret rendezvous with Christ that the soul can say, 'My lover is mine and I am his . . . I found the one my heart loves. I held him and would not let him go . . . My lover is radiant . . . outstanding among ten thousand . . . he is

altogether lovely' (selected from Song of Solomon).
This volume is not written for the hurried person who
is grasping for some media bite along the way, a minute
with Jesus and no more. It is intended for the searching
heart which acknowledges that it is worth giving time
and extended thought in order to see the King in his
beauty.

To behold Jesus, to adore him, and to rejoice in his
praises are not means to higher ends. Fixing the eyes of
our souls upon the Lamb of God, and bowing before
him in joyful, loving worship *is* the highest end of our
existence, the only fully satisfying experience of the
human heart, the chief ingredient of human
blessedness. 'That I may know him . . . ' (*Philippians
3:10*) and enjoy him forever is the end for which every
saint lives.

Perhaps some will read these pages who have never
detected any glory in Jesus Christ. 'He had no beauty
or majesty to attract us to him, nothing in his
appearance that we should desire him' (*Isaiah 53:2*) is
your testimony. You look at the fullest objective
revelation of the Son of God in the New Testament,
but you say, 'Ichabod' – where is the glory? You think
there is nothing special about Christ. You are not
drawn to him.

If you find no loveliness in Christ, that fact should
alarm you. Paul commented about those who, in the
full light of the revealed glory of God, saw no beauty:
'If our gospel is hidden, it is hidden to those who are
perishing. The god of this age has blinded the minds of
unbelievers, so that they cannot see the light of the
gospel of the glory of Christ' (*2 Corinthians 4:3–4*).
When you stand beneath the unclouded noonday sun
but can see no light, it is a shocking exposure of

yourself. You are blind. You cannot see the obvious light. If you detect no wondrous majesty and captivating loveliness in Christ, you are spiritually blind. You are perishing!

'We have seen Jesus' glory, the glory as of the only begotten of the Father, *full* of grace and truth' (*John 1:14*). 'He was in the world, and though the world was made through him, the world did not recognize him' (*John 1:10*). For the blind and undiscerning, more is required than full, plain, objective revelation of the glory of God in the person of Jesus Christ. Along with the divinely given light in Christ before your eyes, the Lord must grant you inward sight to receive the light.

We who are Christians can recall when we heard so much about the Son of God but saw no radiant nobility in him. But 'God, who said, "Let light shine out of darkness," made his light shine *in* our hearts to give us the light of the knowledge of the glory of God in the face of Jesus Christ' (*2 Corinthians 4:6*). The truth of Christ was given to the angry Saul of Tarsus as he dragged Christians off to prison. The splendour of Christ was set before Saul. But this man talks about another day 'when God was pleased to reveal his Son *in* me' (*Galatians 1:15,16*).

If any who see no glory in Christ Jesus read these pages about him, my prayer is that he who commanded light to shine out of darkness in the first creation will, in connection with the objective revelations of Scripture, shine in your heart to give you, in a new creation work, the knowledge of the glory of God. This glory is in the face of Jesus Christ. May you see it. May God who has revealed his Son *to* you be pleased to reveal his Son *in* you.

Three thousand years ago the Lord prepared a poet to give us remarkable revelations about Jesus, the Messiah. The poet's colourful life equipped him with vivid impressions of the ancient world. He experienced the noise and confusion of ancient battle fields. The quiet majesty and awesome power of the eastern monarch's throne room were familiar to him as well. He was equally at home as a humble shepherd, gathering a flock of sheep around him beneath the impressive glories of the heavens. Widely diverse experiences were gathered up into the poet's mind and formed the resources of his talent of hymn writing.

David's psalms employ such grand imagery. Yet all the fascinating word-pictures are used to express what his eyes of faith had seen of Christ. His subject is not ancient ways of war, government and husbandry. The psalms are pointing and crying, 'Behold your God!' As the ancient artist strained his genius to the limit, the effort was carried along by the Holy Spirit. His hymns are breathed out by God. Using David's talent, the words of God reveal our holy Lord.

May God grant that the readers of this volume may see Jesus in their inmost being, may embrace Christ by divinely given faith, and seeing the Lord, may they rejoice with joy unspeakable and full of glory.

Psalm 2

A PHILOSOPHY OF LIFE

'For to me, to live is Christ . . .'

(Philippians 1:21)

Because God made us intelligent creatures, every man and woman has a philosophy of life. An ill-educated, violent gang member from a modern city's ghetto has a set of beliefs which interpret his experiences and guide his actions. His outlook on life may not be critically studied or logically consistent like the perspective of a university professor. Yet each of us has impressions of who he is and of the nature of the world in which he lives, and these convictions guide his behaviour, and form his understanding of life.

David artistically moulded his philosophy into four word-pictures, each being three verses in length. In Psalm 2, four rapidly given verbal slides present us with David's world view. They are not disjointed scenes but form a unified mural. The four impressions have a single message. They are tied together with a central figure who appears in each of the scenes. At the focal point in each scene is the Christ who is called in vs. 2 God's 'Anointed One', in vs. 6 God's chosen 'King', in vss. 7 and 12 God's 'Son'. 'Messiah' is the Hebrew term for the English 'Anointed One', and for the Greek word 'Christ'.

Psalm 2 does not identify its author. But the New Testament does tell us who composed this compact, yet profound philosophy. Acts 4:25 and 26 reveal that it was 'God through the mouth of his servant David who said' these words. They are David's words. They are God's words; for God sovereignly controlled David's composition of Psalm 2. David spoke. But God spoke through his mouth, using his talent, employing his mental and spiritual processes to produce divine truth. David's poem bears the authority of heaven. Its impressions of reality correspond perfectly with reality itself. Here is a world view you should adopt; for it is true.

Quaint customs of ancient times are suggested in the imagery of the second psalm. Nevertheless, beneath cultural incidentals you will find the analysis in David's hymn amazingly up-to-date. For all the heralding of modern advances, you will be compelled to conclude that the basic issues of life are now as they have always been. Really important matters in this world have remained unchanged since 1,000 BC.

With the simplicity of a few poetic brush strokes David will explain all the upheavals of our century. He will tell you where they will all end. And as you look closely you will find your own face in his mural. You have a personal interest and involvement in each scene. The first three define the predicament for you and all mankind. The fourth calls upon you for decisive action. There is a note of urgency and pleading lest you miss the way by adopting a wrong and ruinous philosophy. We have seen that the advice of this psalm carries both the weight of human wisdom and that of divine counsel. If you do not adopt it as your outlook on life, there is a day coming in which you will look back upon life with this viewpoint.

SCENE 1: THE MUTINY OF MAN, OR CHRIST
REJECTED

*'Why do the nations rage and the peoples plot in vain?
The kings of the earth take their stand and the rulers
gather together against the Lord and against his
Anointed One. "Let us break their chains," they say,
"and throw off their fetters."'*

Psalm 2:1–3

To the eye of David, the great general of Israel's forces,
this world is an enormous battlefield. Skilled at recon-
naissance, the son of Jesse glances at massive movements
of armies. Many would see only confusion, but he
recognizes at once the critical details and reduces all to
an uncomplicated analysis.

Verse 1 describes the troops assembling for war.
Verse 2 details the officers' preparations for combat.
They set their various regiments in battle formation and
then meet for a council of war. Immediately in their
strategy session the rulers name their enemy. Verse 3
records the actual words of the plotting military commanders, expressing the objective of their conflict.

This world is a vast plain on to which a gigantic army
is forming. With differing uniforms 'the nations' gather
– all the nations of the earth; all past, present and future
kingdoms of this world. All members of the human race
from all times are on the march. In all the dust raised by
staggering numbers, do not miss a very special person.
You are in the midst of this theatre of war. You are a
combatant!

The Hebrew word David uses to describe the conven-
ing military machine is difficult to translate with one
English equivalent. The King James Version uses 'rage'.

There is violence or noisy hostility in the gathering, as you might expect when men are spoiling for a fight. Shouts of anger and boasts of the coming assault penetrate the air. The *N.I.V.* has chosen to translate the word 'conspire'. Although there is noise and seeming chaos on the battleground, the venom of common hatred and unified zeal to attack creates an order after all. Perhaps the best translation is that the nations 'tumultuously assemble'.

These individual warriors are not soldiers of fortune, seeking only adventure and wealth. They are not ignorant conscripts compelled to fight in a war whose purpose they do not understand. For as the nations surge onto the field of combat, 'the peoples plot'. They believe in this war. They share agreement with their rulers as to the purpose for the coming fray. Enthusiasm for the united objective produces the noise and energy with which all humanity musters.

We have noticed it too. A deep disquiet rumbles through our world. Convulsive activity, frantic movement, and hysterical voices punctuate our generation. Each segment of human endeavour is a boiling cauldron of turbulence. Politics, academia, business, religion, entertainment and the military contribute to the restive clatter of our times. There seems to be no peace for our weary souls. All is motion and noise. No wonder we are confused by the unsettled condition of our planet.

Yet David is not befuddled. There is a unifying explanation, an organizing principle to all the dashing and blaring of both past and present history. It is a factor which ties all of life into our own personal thoughts and actions. For all of our variety in culture, personality, age, station and locality, mankind is eager to participate in a universal campaign. Intelligent enthusiasm carries us all into the fight. The contrived attack explains your existence and that of your neighbours. We are in a universal crusade!

At the centre of this tumultuous assembly the rulers are taking counsel together. There are 'the kings of the earth', so treacherous in envy and competition towards one another. Yet they have found a common cause. Marxist rulers and democrats, liberal and conservative, communist and capitalist are all agreed in this one kernel of purpose. They are all united with the one plot that invigorates the teeming nations. Their council gives expression to the great ambition of every human heart.

It is from eavesdropping on the strategy session that we have the first indication of the enemy against whom the entire human race wishes to fight. The kings identify the hated object of their rage. We shall take aim 'against the Lord (Jehovah) and against his Anointed One (Christ)'.

No wonder David began his hymn with the word 'Why?' It was not a 'why' of puzzlement, but one of indignation and astonishment. He is shocked. It is all so senseless! So bizarre! 'The peoples plot *in vain*' (*vs. 1*). What absurdity to declare war on the living God and his Messiah! Yet this antagonism merges all mankind into one co-ordinated militia. It explains human thought and human action.

Have you ever picked up your newspaper to scan the stories of the day and thought that our world is a confusing jumble? Have you wondered if there is any thread of meaning to sew together the widely diverse happenings of our age? Have you been unable to give any explanation to it all?

David tells you, 'I have discovered the key to every part of human history.' There is one mainspring that moves the senator in halls of government and the prostitute on the street. I know what the business man on Wall Street and the homeless drug addict have in common. I can tell you the driving motive shared by the Chinese school teacher, the Marxist guerrilla in Africa and the American athlete. All of them hate the true and living God and are spurred by a passion to destroy his Messiah. All – all of humanity – is galvanized for rebellion! It is shocking to the point of being unbelievable, but it is true.

On only one occasion Jehovah became flesh and dwelt among us on earth in the person of his Son, the Lord Jesus Christ. This was mankind's only opportunity to lay its hands on the Lord from heaven. At that moment all humanity rose up as one to crucify the Anointed of the Lord. Political rivals (Herod and Pilate) agreed to put Jesus to death. Jews and Gentiles laboured side by side in this project. Religious competitors (Herodians, Pharisees, Sadducees and heathen) co-operated fully to crucify the Son of God. In one unique show of human unity all voices cried, 'Crucify him', 'Away with this man', 'We have no king but Caesar.' With complete solidarity they spat on him, beat him, impaled him, and as his lifeblood drained into the earth, they hatefully mocked him.

Many lessons are taught us by the cross of Calvary. One which no one can fail to recognize is the deep malice which is found in the human spirit. There is a dark, vicious depravity in the human heart which focuses its corrupt passions against the Lord and his Messiah. The pernicious mischief is joyfully attempted deicide.

As you consider the cross of Jesus Christ, you may in your mind quickly distance yourself from those who once afflicted our Lord with a mixture of excruciating pain and ridicule. You believe you would never participate in such a shameful mob action. You are not aware that you have ever hated God. To the contrary, you are conscious of only warm, positive thoughts toward the Almighty and his Son. You cannot agree with David's assessment of this world. At least you and your friends are exceptions to this madness depicted in Psalm 2. You may have your faults, but hostility to God and Christ has not been one of them. You are not aware of having volunteered for service in a brigade marching off to bombard God's palace. Nor did you lampoon the suffering Son of God at the cross.

It is still too soon to reach a firm conclusion on these questions: Is this base enmity against God and his Anointed One universal within humanity? Do I share in the guilt of this unspeakable atrocity? There is yet further evidence which David brings forward to support his philosophy of life. We must consider the actual words on the lips of 'the kings of the earth' gathered in their council of war. This quote expresses the rationale for molesting God and his Messiah. 'Let us break their chains,' they say, 'and throw off their fetters' (*vs. 3*).

Rulers of the earth have reached a consensus. This unanimity of objective in combat is popular, for it represents the conspiracy (*vs. 1*) of each and every warrior. All are determined to overthrow the authority of God and his Christ. God's rule and government over mankind is viewed as restrictive and oppressive. God's rules or laws are unwanted. Terms are chosen which are charged with nasty anger and contempt.

'Chains' and 'fetters' are accusatory words, suggesting that God is harsh and unfair, his Son is severe and cruel. God's commandments are considered an insufferable bondage.

Quite a few have kindly thoughts toward God because they have created a god in their imaginations. He is only a god of love and benevolence to them. All of his power or control of the world is held in store to respond to their requests. But never would they think of their god making demands of them! They may always seek help from their all-kind heavenly gentleman (their cosmic genie). He is a servant-god exercising his power to do their will, but never asserting his will with requirements of them. No wonder then that so many have only warm and friendly emotions toward the god of their fantasy.

When the God of Scripture arises into view, the very same individuals have exceedingly different responses to him. They do not love a holy God who maintains a righteous government over the children of men. They are not sympathetic to the pure moral commandments which the Lord of heaven published for the regulation of human affairs. Realization that the holy Judge of all the earth is determined to enforce his perfect law produces both alarm and hostility. If men and women are told that God maintains absolute dominion over this earth to bring moral justice to all, they may feel inward rebellion.

Women cannot abide God's assigning them a different role in society from the one he has appointed for men. Nor will many endure any law from God that protects human life within the mother's womb. Men will not tolerate a law from God restricting their sexual activity to the female sex and that only within the confines of marriage. All of these produce deep hostility, anger, clenched fists held high against God, his laws, his Bible.

Society becomes violently hostile if anyone sincerely proposes that God was serious in making Sabbath-keeping a moral requirement for all men. What a bondage to lose sporting events and other pleasures for even one day per week! We will not have the God of the Ten Commandments to reign over us. Off they go to volunteer in the rebellion. Surely God is not serious in forbidding us to take his name on our lips as an empty jest or thoughtless oath. That would be too restrictive. He cannot really mean that we must be strictly honest on all occasions!

If men could strip God of his law-making powers, they would gladly have him and his Crown-Prince, Jesus, for figurehead royalty. If we could reshape his kingdom to our modern ideals and dictate to him how he should do the job of 'god', it would be quite all right. He may be loving and compassionate, even miracle-working in our interests but not morally demanding. When it becomes clear that he intends to make the laws of our world and to enforce them, none – not one – will have his rule.

There is in every man, deeply-imbedded, a stubborn refusal of God's authority. When God's law comes into view this arrogant pride breaks into malicious and open defiance. It is just what Paul noted, man's 'mind does not submit to God's law, nor can it do so' (*Romans 8:7*). It is in a state of enmity towards God. It is this that you have in common with all other human beings. Refined socialite and skid-row alcoholic, respected scholar and hated pick-pocket are alike part of this mutiny against heaven, this high treason against the throne of God, this war for independence from the Most High, his Messiah, and his law.

Can it be that you have never thought deeply enough about your sin? You would surely admit that you have broken God's commandments. You have even secretly wished that the Ten Commandments did not exist, so that you could be 'free' to act out your desires to your heart's content. In better moments you have realized that your sins have led to trouble and sorrow for yourself. Beyond this your evil words and acts have inflicted pain on others around you. Although both of these observations are accurate we have not yet seen in them the depths of sin. The truly shocking and disgusting aspect of your sin and mine is that every transgression is a deed of contempt for God and his Son.

The Almighty who made us and gave us every faculty and power we possess is the intended victim of the crime of sin. The most hideous and wrong thing about any sin is that it is a malicious arrow aimed at the Lord of glory. This is the obnoxious and intolerable ingredient of our sin, the scandal of our human race.

David was compelled to awaken to this heartbreaking reality in his own life. He impregnated Bathsheba while she was another man's wife, bringing to *her* great anxiety and disgrace. He murdered Uriah, her husband, to escape his vengeance, a great injustice against the *man*. But when Nathan the prophet confronted David he declared from God's mouth, 'You have despised *me*' (*2 Samuel 12:10*). This piercing accusation exposed the gruesome baseness of his sin and caused the sinner to cry to God in Psalm 51:4: 'Against *you*, *you* only, have I sinned and done what is evil in *your* sight.'

We are complacent in sin only because in error we think of God's law as containing arbitrary and abstract standards detached from himself. In truth his commandments are a revelation of his own character, an extension of his very Being. Our transgressions of the law only register the deep inward disdain we have for the infinitely wise, holy, righteous, just and loving God.

Alas, it is a universal sedition, an ugly and loathsome secret of our humanity. The driving force which explains life on this planet is rebellion against God our Maker. 'Why?' What criminal insanity lurks in the whole fabric of human living! The plain truth about us when it is spoken clearly is monstrous madness. It is outrageous. We are depraved and corrupt. We are thankless and vile.

Our predicament is perilous. What is to become of us? individually? as a unified army? David's philosophy is only begun.

SCENE 2: THE SUPREMACY OF GOD, OR CHRIST APPOINTED

'The One enthroned in heaven laughs; the Lord scoffs at them. Then he rebukes them in his anger and terrifies them in his wrath, saying, "I have installed my King on Zion, my holy hill."'

Psalm 2:4–6

David's second word-picture stands in surprising contrast with his first. Instead of the earth teeming with multitudes of creatures, the poet portrays heaven and a solitary divine figure in it. In place of the crude noises of a battlefield has come the calm dignity of a throne room.

Psalm 2: A Philosophy of Life

The sweet psalmist of Israel has transported us infinitely far above battle-ground-earth, to where the Most High conducts his affairs of state. His Divine Majesty is completely aware of all that is occurring in this world. His omniscience scans the 'vain plottings' within the minds of the people (*vs. 1*). His eye penetrates the top-secret councils of world leaders (*vs. 2*). Immediately the Lord knows that his subjects are in universal rebellion against his holy rule. They are implacable in their hatred toward him and his Messiah. As in scene 1 the kings of the earth spoke to express their aims in this war, so in scene 2 the King of kings declares his mind concerning this conflict.

Even more startling than the entire human race declaring war on the Almighty is the Lord's response of *laughter*! It is not a laugh of amusement or delight. David has shown us that anger covers the King's countenance and wrath rides upon his every word. This laughter expresses contempt and scoffing. The laughter arises from God's impregnable supremacy.

Jehovah's throne remains unshaken by all that human animosity can do. After man's intellect has invented its most brilliant assaults, and after all the force and energy of all human creatures who ever have lived or will live has been combined into a single thrust against God and his Messiah, God is untouched, unharmed, unthreatened, unhindered, unchanged in his person, his position, and his plans.

It is absurd for clay to fight the Potter. It is futile for creatures of dust to war against the infinite Spirit. They plot in vain (*vs. 1*). 'His wisdom is profound, his power is vast. Who has resisted him and come out unscathed?' (*Job 9:4*). 'Why' (*vs. 1*) have they undertaken the laughable? There is laughter in heaven! God is perfectly at ease upon his throne. Heaven's gates do not even rattle. 'There is no wisdom, no insight, no plan that can succeed against the Almighty' (*Proverbs 21:30*).

A massive army is on the march against him, but the One enthroned in heaven does not show the least uneasiness. There is displeasure but not panic. The Lord does not even change direction in his management of the earth. There are not even any fresh initiatives to meet a crisis. God speaks only of what he has already done. His decrees of long ago will stand. He has already installed a King over the earth. He has spoken already and his purpose will prevail against men and devils. Their opposition to his will is outrageous. It is laughable.

'Surely the nations are like a drop in a bucket [to God]; they are regarded [by him] as dust on the scales; . . . Before him all the nations are as nothing; they are regarded by him as worthless and less than nothing . . . He sits enthroned above the circle of the earth, and its people are like grasshoppers . . . He brings princes to naught and reduces the rulers of this world to nothing' (*Isaiah 40:15–23*).

It is a joke that man plots to overthrow God's authority. Can a flea attack an elephant? Shall a rabbit fight with a lion? Have you ever seen a toddler fall into a rage against a muscular man and begin to pummel him? What does the adult do? He laughs. A child cannot injure the man of war. The one united crusade of mankind is destined to utter failure. God is a rock who will not be moved.

With tones of mocking and derision toward the weakling warriors of the earth the Supreme Potentate announces his answer to human rebellion against his rule and his law. 'I have installed my King.' He has unilaterally appointed Christ to rule over all the earth. The coronation is accomplished. 'Our God is in heaven; he does whatever pleases him' (*Psalm 115:3*). He does it in defiance of the deepest wishes of men, the most insistent objections of men, the violent and noisy opposition of men.

Christ was sent into the world to be a King, God's chosen mediatorial King. At his trial and crucifixion Jesus' kingship was a dominant issue. Soldiers mimicked reverence to the Jewish King. Pilate asked the Jews if he should crucify their King while Hebrew observers denied that he was their King. In contempt for their nation and their religion Pilate commanded that a sign hang over Jesus announcing him to be the King of the Jews. At Golgotha all the world was sending a message to the Lord who sent his Son, Jesus, into this world. In the words of Luke 19:14 it was, 'We don't want this man to be our King.'

But the Maker of heaven and earth never requested human suffrage for the reign of his Son. Man's opinion was never asked. A vote was never taken. It was the Lord of Hosts who installed Jesus as King. Never were men asked to 'make Jesus their Lord'. A choice was not given. It was his prerogative as Ruler of the universe to appoint the King.

Divine sovereignty was not undermined by Jesus' crucifixion, it was forcefully accentuated. While all mankind denied that Jesus was a King, indeed, while they voiced extreme displeasure at the thought of his being a King, the One enthroned in heaven installed Jesus as King. '*God* has made this Jesus, whom you crucified, both Lord and Christ' (*Acts 2:36*). Our gospel does not beg men and women to make Jesus

Lord. It triumphantly announces that Jehovah has settled that issue. For our God 'works out everything in conformity with the purpose of his will' (*Ephesians 1:11*). 'He does as he pleases with the powers of heaven and the peoples of the earth. No one can hold back his hand or say to him: "What have you done?"' (*Daniel 4:35*).

Millions upon millions of men and women are agitated, conspiring, tumultuous, warring. Their foe is a calm solitary figure speaking one word from a dignified throne. His word always accomplishes the end for which it is spoken. Jesus Christ is the Lord, the King over all. God said it. It is so!

Christ is installed on 'my holy hill' (*vs. 6*). Everything associated with the person and reign of the Anointed One is characterized by holiness. It was Jesus' perfect embodiment of pure moral integrity and his insistence upon administering the holy law of God which made him the object of man's bitter, hateful rejection (*vs. 3*). Because God has made him Lord, holiness will triumph in the earth. Jesus' imperial sway issues from a position of holiness. He is pledged to uphold the very system of righteousness which fallen mankind instinctively despises.

This Jesus is the King of glory. Of course glory refers to beauty or splendour. His is the beauty of holiness. He is the spotless Lamb of God, the sinless One who always did what pleased his Father. His holiness qualified him to be the one perfect sacrifice for our sins, acceptable to an infinitely pure God. He is 'holy' (completely devoted to God the Father, perfectly obeying the first four commandments), 'harmless' (never injuring his fellow men, perfectly keeping the last six commandments), 'undefiled' (having no evil within himself), 'separate from sinners' (utterly unlike all other men morally) (*Hebrews 7:26*).

Jesus' teaching focused on the subject of righteousness. Those who heard him were taught that 'unless your righteousness surpasses that of the Pharisees and the teachers of the law, you will certainly not enter the kingdom of heaven' (*Matthew 5:20*). He emphasized the spirituality of God's holy law. Anger without cause is murder in the heart. Looking upon a woman lustfully is adultery in the heart. Love must extend even to enemies. Worship must arise from true devotion in the soul, or it is not acceptable to God. 'Seek *first* his kingdom and his *righteousness*' (*Matthew 6:33*). 'Not everyone who *says* to me, "Lord, Lord," will enter the kingdom of heaven, but only he who *does* the will of my Father in heaven' (*Matthew 7:21*). Evil doers will be sent away from the presence of the king upon his *holy* hill.

The subject of Jesus' gospel was righteousness. What he offered to those who trust him is the righteousness of God. Paul said, 'I am not ashamed of the gospel of Christ . . . for in it the righteousness of God is revealed' (*Romans 1:16,17*). Our Saviour Jesus Christ 'gave himself for us to redeem us from all wickedness and to purify for himself a people that are his very own, eager to do what is good' (*Titus 2:14*). He purchased for his people and sent to them the *Holy* Spirit who transforms them, 'that the righteous requirement of the law might be fulfilled in us who . . . walk . . . according to the Spirit' (*Romans 8:4*). This Spirit writes God's law upon the hearts of Jesus' disciples (*Hebrews 8:10*).

As Lord of all, Jesus will bring into existence 'a new heaven and a new earth, the home of righteousness' (*2 Peter 3:13*) in hope of which his people now 'make every effort to be spotless, blameless' (*2 Peter 3:14*). 'Nothing impure will ever enter it, nor will anyone who does what is shameful or deceitful' (*Revelation 21:27*). His kingdom will be inhabited only by those who have his own righteousness imputed *to* them, and a Spirit-produced righteousness *in* them.

The leading feature of Jesus' dominion is holiness. He is enthroned on a holy hill. Every facet of his person and government sparkles with the beauty of holiness. As he reigns, righteousness triumphs in the earth, among the sons of men.

This holy hill, identified as the seat of Messiah's holy kingship, is called 'Zion'. Zion was a hill which David captured from the Jebusites. It became the centre for worship and the seat of government for the people of God in David's day. Just so 'Zion' is taken up in the New Testament as a symbolic name for the Church of Jesus Christ (*Hebrews 12:22–24*). All gospel believers are built upon the precious and chosen cornerstone laid in Zion (*1 Peter 2:6*). The Church of Jesus Christ is now the centre of true spiritual worship and the seat of Jesus' holy reign on the earth.

Just as the Lord Jesus was despised and rejected by men and jeered at as a King, so too is the Church which is faithful to Biblical truth and righteousness. 'If they persecuted me, they will persecute you also' (*John 15:20*). The army assembled against Jehovah and his Christ are angry with the lifestyle and message of the Church. The people of God uphold God's righteous law by their teachings and by their example. The hill of Zion is a holy hill. Its inhabitants are saints (*holy ones*). Christians have been 'called to be saints' (*Romans 1:7*).

This mutinous humanity dismisses the Church as irrelevant and ineffective. It did not understand or appreciate the spiritual, righteous operations of the

Son of God as he established his kingdom in the hearts of men. They crucified the Lord of glory. Still, men of the earth cannot discern the infinite power unleashed by Jesus Christ in the transformation of one soul. There is no appreciation of the Spirit working through the gospel to change radically the moral character of men. But this is the only force at work in our world with a hopeful future. Here, in Zion's holy hill, the reign of Christ has begun. Of his kingdom there shall be no end. His dominion is an everlasting dominion.

To Christ and his Church belong the world, the future, all things. He will reign until all enemies have been subjected under his feet. The working of God's mighty strength 'he exerted in Christ when he raised him from the dead and seated him at his right hand in the heavenly realms, far above all rule and authority, power and dominion, and every title that can be given, not only in the present age but also in the one to come. And God placed all things under his feet and appointed him to be head over everything *for the church*, which is his body . . . ' (*Ephesians 1:19–23*). The One enthroned in heaven laughed at man's rebellion and said, 'I have installed my King on Zion, my holy hill' (*vs. 6*).

Fearful Christian, how we tend to quiver when the world rattles its sabres. Its mocking alone can make us afraid. We need to lift our eyes above the battlefield earth with its impotent rebellion against Jehovah and his Christ. The foundation of our world is in a quiet throne room in heaven. 'Be still, and know that I am God; I will be exalted *among the nations*, I will be exalted *in the earth*' (*Psalm 46:10*). 'I have installed my King' (*vs. 6*). The appointed King is reigning in his Church, on Zion's holy hill. God's purposes are standing fast. His plan for the world is in no jeopardy. His King is reigning and his kingdom is being built on schedule, despite the raucous rebels of the earth.

SCENE 3: THE AUTHORITY OF CHRIST, OR CHRIST COMMISSIONED

'I will proclaim the decree of the Lord: He said to me, "You are my Son; today I have begotten you. Ask of me, and I will make the nations your inheritance, the ends of the earth your possession. You will rule them with an iron sceptre; you will dash them to pieces like pottery."'

Psalm 2:7–9

A third verbal slide flashes on the screen in David's gripping poetic presentation. Already he has left deep impressions about the meaning of our existence. We are awake to the significance of our lives, our world, our future. The ancient poet-king has shown us sinful, rebellious man and the unshaken, sovereign and holy God. Insights into God's character and purposes have been given to us. But it is time for yet another element of David's philosophy of life.

There is no startling change in moving from scene two to scene three. The contrasts between the first two visions were dramatic. These verses are a further development of what David began to show us in the heavenly palace of Jehovah. Here we continue in a stately throne room. Tranquillity and dignity, intelligent purpose and power dominate the atmosphere.

However, a new figure has appeared. No longer are we looking at Jehovah upon his throne. For the first time we are gazing full into the face of God's 'Anointed One' (*vs.2*), the King installed on Zion, God's holy hill

[30]

(*vs. 6*). Already we have heard men speak of him in scene 1 and God speak of him in scene 2. Now the time has come to usher us into the presence of His Majesty, the Lord Jesus.

Little needs to be said of Messiah's lofty position, for this has already been described for us. Whereas a description of the Lord dominated scene 2, and God's words were recorded only in verse 6, this entire section (*vss. 7–9*) is filled with the words of the enthroned Christ. He explains to us the ultimate origin and ultimate end of his regency.

Although the Lord Jesus is the spokesman from his mediatorial throne, the words are mostly the words of Jehovah himself repeated to us by Messiah. 'I will proclaim the decree of Jehovah' which he delivered to me at my coronation. These words of Jehovah to his Anointed One, spoken as he placed a crown on his head, contain the commission of the newly installed King. It is his mandate, defining the scope of his mission, the design for regal action on the part of the Christ of God.

'He said to me' . . . and afterward follow the exact words of Jehovah. How like our Lord Jesus Christ who came down from heaven not to do his own will but to do the will of him who sent him (*John 6:38*). In carrying out the divinely given mission, this Messiah spoke the very words of God. 'I gave them the words you gave me' (*John 17:8*). He is the faithful Servant of the Lord, carefully executing the will of his God and repeating his very words. He and the Father completely shared one mind and one will regarding his Messianic reign.

A theological dispute has centred upon the first words of Jehovah which Messiah quotes to us. 'You are my Son; today I have begotten you' (*vs. 7*). A controversy continues over whether the phrase 'I have begotten you' refers to God the Son being eternally begotten by God the Father, or whether it refers to the resurrection of Jesus Christ from the dead.

Those who believe that the reference is to the resurrection point out that the Apostle Paul while preaching in a synagogue at Pisidian Antioch quoted this text in connection with the fact that God raised Jesus from the dead (*Acts 13:33*). They also note that Jesus 'was declared with power to be the Son of God by his resurrection from the dead' (*Romans 1:4*). Furthermore it was in conjunction with Jesus' resurrection that our Lord announced, 'All authority in heaven and on earth has been given to me' (*Matthew 28:18*). Also, resurrection is the proof that Jesus will judge the world with justice (*Acts 17:31*). Hence those who hold this view believe God's words apply the 'today' of verse 7 to the day on which he raised Jesus from the dead, that being the day he was installed as the King.

Those taking the view that 'I have begotten you' must refer to the Father eternally begetting the Son cite the use of this text in Hebrews 1:5, in which the divine character of God's Son is being emphasized. They would interpret 'today' of verse 7 as being spoken in eternity and referring to no specific day in history. The Father's declaration would have attended his decree from eternity.

In one sense the controversy is not critical. Both sides believe in the full divinity of the Messiah, including his being eternally begotten by the Father. Both believe that Jesus' divinity was powerfully published by his resurrection from the dead. The controversy merely surrounds which Biblical truth is being taught by Psalm 2:7.

In either event, 'You are my Son, today I have begotten you' forms a preamble to the commissioning of the Anointed One as King. The mouth of the Lord identifies the person of the Messiah with the loftiest dignity. The Christ is none other than the Son of the living God (*Matthew 16:16*). The One enthroned in heaven acknowledges that his appointed monarch shares equally in his divinity. This identification of the One whom we are beholding in scene 3 is held by the Almighty in the deepest imaginable affection. 'You are my Son' signifies an intimate relationship between the two persons. They have a fellowship of wondrous love. Whether the last phrase 'Today I have begotten you' declares the mysterious eternal relationship between these two persons of the holy Trinity or speaks of the mighty publication of their relationship through Jesus' resurrection, it only intensifies the expression of the Father's loving approval of and proud identification with his Son.

From the commendation of the King in verse 7, the Father passes on to the specific commission of his reign. Verse 8 defines the extent of Messiah's royal jurisdiction while verse 9 assigns a final purpose to his government.

Jehovah will convey to his Son all the nations of mankind. They will be his inheritance, his portion. The very same insurgent nations depicted in verse 1 belong to him. Restive, seditious hordes are utterly under his power, and subject to his wish. All the ends of the earth are granted to Messiah as his estate. Absolute sovereignty over the earth and the human race is his legacy. It is divinely given. None can contest his right to do with them as he pleases. All power in heaven and upon the earth as it touches earth and humanity is in the hands of the Anointed One. Christ's full dominion extends to your nation, your town, your life. 'The ends of the earth' are his possession!

An interesting truth is taught by the form in which Jehovah makes his decree. He intends to endow the Son with complete authority over men and earth. Yet the Lord says, 'Ask of me, and I will make the nations your inheritance.' Although the Lord of hosts has purposed to install the Son and has decreed that his reign will surely come to pass, it is his will that this shall occur through the means of prayer. Jesus, the mediatorial King, must pray as he did in John 17: 1–5, and in response Jehovah will consign to the Son's plenary authority all the earth and its inhabitants. The God who ordains the end ordains the means to the end in his inscrutable sovereignty.

All who worship and serve the Son of God are delighted at the vast extent of his dominion. 'Worthy is the Lamb, who was slain, to receive power and wealth and wisdom and strength and honour and glory and praise!' (*Revelation 5:12*). We fall down and worship him upon his mediatorial throne of limitless power.

However, the final words of Jehovah's transfer of powers to the Messiah are terrifying. They were intended to be so. Installation of God's King upon his holy hill was an act of angry rebuke and terrifying wrath to intransigent nations (*vs. 5*). As Lord of the nations and King of all the ends of the earth, Messiah must dispense holy justice to riotous sinners. The Anointed must be Judge and Executioner over the wicked. After all, this installation was announced in the context of an insurrection by the nations. God's decree to Messiah includes his final deposition of defiant revolutionaries.

Messiah is seated upon a throne. In his hand is a sceptre, an ornamented staff symbolic of imperial authority. Christ's sceptre is iron. It is more than symbolic. It will be wielded with angry force against the errant nations. His weapon is iron. Their constitution is as fragile as a potter's vessel. If the iron sceptre strikes the clay figurines of human nature they will be dashed to pieces. Irreparable destruction must result for frail, brittle enemies of this throne.

Scripture takes up this view of Messiah ruling with an iron sceptre once more in its vivid description of the final judgment: 'I saw heaven standing open and there before me was a white horse, whose rider is called Faithful and True. With justice he judges and makes war. His eyes are like blazing fire, and on his head are many crowns . . . He is dressed in a robe dipped in blood, and his name is the Word of God. The armies of heaven were following him, riding on white horses and dressed in fine linen, white and clean. Out of his mouth comes a sharp sword with which to strike down *the nations. "He will rule them with an iron sceptre."* He treads the winepress of the fury of the wrath of God Almighty. On his robe and on his thigh he has the name written: KING OF KINGS AND LORD OF LORDS' (*Revelation 19: 11–16*).

At the last day the Lord Jesus will be 'revealed from heaven in blazing fire with his powerful angels. He will punish those who do not know God and do not obey the gospel of our Lord Jesus. They will be punished with everlasting destruction . . . ' (*2 Thessalonians 1:7–9*). In his office as King Messiah must bring final judgment upon the nations which are anarchists toward God's holy law, haters of God's holy Person, and at war against God's holy Son. He is God's deputy sovereign to execute wrath with a sceptre of iron.

Into the power of the Son has been given the final disposition of justice upon the earth. He has authority and might to assign men and nations their irrevocable destinies. The only appropriate response of sinners to a display of his holy majesty is to fear and tremble. His throne is terrifying to the ungodly. His reign is the vehicle of the wrath of Almighty God to rebels. Holy vengeance and divine fury await the nations. Who can stand when he appears in the day of terror?

These first three scenes of David's mural of our existence have been calculated to heighten your consciousness of the most profound realities of this world. You have been born as a member of the mutinous nations. You were born with a seditious heart of hatred to God. Your disaffection toward God's holy law indicates that your moral crimes helped to crucify the Lord of glory. Your sins are against Jehovah and his Messiah.

Jehovah's response to the entire insurgency of mankind, of which you are a part, has been to carry on calmly with his eternal purpose to install a King upon his holy hill, Zion. This expedient would sufficiently express divine wrath against earthly rebels.

God's precious Son is now upon a throne which holds sway over all affairs of earth and humankind. He has been invested with power and authority and directed by express, divine instructions to smash to pieces with a rod of iron the delicate humanity impatient of God's holy rule. The destruction of rebel nations is destined. It is approaching; Jehovah's Son is on his throne, sceptre in hand.

What can you do to escape impending wrath? Under these awful elements of reality, what shall you do? You face a most desperate crisis. Is there any escape from the wrath of the Lamb? Is your only possible strategy to call upon mountains and rocks to fall on you and hide you from the face of him who sits on the throne? (*Revelation 6:16*). Is there any relief from the crushing terror David has placed upon our consciences with his cogent poetry? If your spirit begins to feel these questions, the Lord has prepared you to welcome a final word-picture.

SCENE 4: THE POLICY OF THE GOSPEL, OR CHRIST RECEIVED

'*Therefore, you kings, be wise; be warned, you rulers of the earth. Serve the Lord with fear and rejoice with trembling. Kiss the Son, lest he be angry and you be destroyed in your way, for his wrath can flare up in a moment. Blessed are all who take refuge in him.*'

Psalm 2:10–12

David's fourth and final poetic sketch brings us his emphatic conclusions about human life and the nature of our world. Again we are in the throne room. This should not surprise us. The Son of Jesse was a king. His familiar habitat was the courts of monarchs. Besides, the psalmist has tailored his song for use with his peers. He speaks directly to 'kings' and 'rulers of the earth' (*vs. 10*) just as we would instinctively orient our witness to those who share our station and calling in life.

Once more the Son is upon the throne in verses 10–12, but he is not alone. Now David is the spokesman (not rulers of nations as in verse 3 or Jehovah as in verse

6 or the Anointed One as in verses 7–9). David is serving as guide to the judgment hall of Messiah. He is leading earthly dignitaries into the presence of Jehovah's King installed on Zion. As he ushers temporal princes into their audience with the Inheritor of Nations and Possessor of the Ends of the Earth, David advises them upon the proper protocol of this court. Kings of the earth are instructed how best to behave themselves before His Majesty, the Christ, the Son of the living God. How may they approach him who sits upon the throne at God's right hand? What ought they to say in order to obtain a favourable interview?

Here is the enormous contrast in the final section of Psalm 2. There is a ray of hope! All that has led up to this point has frightened us to the depths of our being. Scenes 1 to 3 have intimidated us, filling us with apprehension and anxiety. But had David not drawn out for us the fundamental truths of our sinful rebellion against Jehovah and his Messiah and the divine response of omnipotent wrath against sinners, we would not be prepared to hear his account of the gospel.

This is what the Scripture means by a conviction of sin. A leading work of the Holy Spirit is to 'convict the world of sin' (*John 16:8*). It is an operation of God's Spirit upon the hearts of unconverted men and women which is absolutely necessary to prepare them for conversion. Until rebels against God's law realize their plight, the gospel will be unappealing to them. David has made us aware that we bear the extreme guilt of having provoked God, the Maker of heaven and earth, with personal affronts against his character of holiness, against his authority, against his Anointed One. We have participated in a grievous and foolish insurrection against Jehovah. Because of this we stand condemned and cursed with the sentence of omnipotent and inescapable wrath. Fearful destruction awaits us.

Have you ever been convicted of sin? Have you ever been awakened to an awareness that you face the very emergency which David has drawn with such alarming skill? Have you seen your own face in the mural David has given us? Until you do, you will not welcome the advice given by the man after God's own heart in the final frame presented in verses 10–12. The gospel will not appeal to you. You will not follow the wisdom and advice of David until you have personally adopted his world view attended by all the appropriate inward responses of fear and agitation of soul. Without the first three scenes the fourth makes no sense and has no impact. The kings which David leads into the palace of the Son of God have become aware of the realities outlined in verses 1–9. They are awakened to flee the coming wrath! They are convicted of having committed monstrous atrocities against the very throne to which they now appeal. Have you gone with them?

Already there have been hints at the mercy of God. If men are so desperately wicked as David teaches, and if the Almighty is so angry with their brazen effrontery that he is determined to dash them to pieces, why has the judgment not yet fallen? Why is there a delay in Messiah's executing the divine commission of visiting the nations with wrath? How is it that the leading perpetrators of mutiny have opportunity to enter the courts of Messiah and sue for peace?

Jehovah and his Christ are longsuffering. It must be that he does not take any pleasure in the death of the wicked, for he does not hasten to his work of justice. The Almighty is slow to wrath. Since he is untouched by the arrows and spears of man's hatred, it is of no loss for him to be patient. 'He does not leave the guilty unpunished' (*Exodus 34:7*). All the demands of divine justice are certain to fall upon the wicked in due time, all the curses of his holy law will be measured out without fail. Yet mercifully we have not yet been consumed. We may seek the Lord while he may still be found and call upon him while his wrath is held in waiting.

Furthermore we have seen Messiah enthroned upon Zion. There *is* a people of God! There is a Church with whom the Holy One of Israel is identified. They are the objects of his favour. They enjoy his fellowship and serve in his cause of truth and righteousness. Each of Zion's citizens was once a vain plotter (*vs. 1*). In days gone by they too hated God's law and marched to war against his Messiah. Now they dwell on a holy hill and serve a holy Lord. It is possible to escape God's displeasure and certain destruction under his anger! He has postponed the rule by iron sceptre while he gathers a people for his very own. The delay of wrath is for the exercise of mercy and grace.

David, as usher of rebels into the presence of the enthroned Christ, stirs yet greater hope. We hear him encouraging the kings who follow him toward Messiah's chambers, 'Blessed are all who take refuge in him' (*vs. 12*). There *is* a refuge from impending wrath! Praise God, there is a way to escape the iron sceptre and its just but smashing impact. The refuge is 'in him', in 'the Son'. Messiah who will one day terrify the wicked by visiting upon them his devastating wrath is exalted as a Prince also to be a Saviour from wrath. He is the one and only shelter from the coming storm of doom. He is the stronghold of safety to all who are united to him. In him there is refuge!

Psalm 2: A Philosophy of Life

It is possible for those who crucified the Son of God with contempt for Jehovah and his law to be 'blessed'. Think of it! Guilty sinner under the curse of God, it is possible to have God's benediction! There is a way to find true and lasting happiness. Your misery may be lifted and your heart filled with solid gladness and eternal bliss. Such blessedness comes to 'all' who betake themselves to Messiah for refuge. You are watching 'rulers of the earth' flee to him for refuge. They were the leaders of the grand rebellion against Jehovah and the Anointed One. They were in the front ranks of those who crucified the Lord of glory. They were the chief of sinners, the leading war criminals in the march against heaven's gates. David holds out hope to *them*! Who then would not be favourably received by him? 'All' who take refuge in Christ will assuredly be blessed. Then go to him at once. You followed the kings in rebellion. Follow them to the refuge.

Much of David's advice to earthly rulers concerns how a rebel may take refuge in Christ. It is done by going to him. The refuge is 'in him'. You must make personal contact with Jesus, the Son of God. Of course vivid poetic pictures are fine for instruction, but where is he who can make me blessed? If I am to hide myself in him for safety, where may he be found?

Since his crucifixion and resurrection Jesus is no longer upon the earth. You can get no closer to him by going to Palestine where he lived. He is not there. He does not live in churches, not even at the altars in front of some houses of worship. He is not in enquiry rooms at evangelistic services. Christ the Lord is in heaven upon his throne. The only way men of the earth may enter his royal dwelling and petition him is by prayer. His ear is open to sincere, heartfelt requests made from the earth. When a sinner seeks refuge in Jesus and longs for blessing instead of cursing, he must pour out the desires of his heart in prayer.

Again David is teaching us how to form the needed prayer for refuge in the one and only Messiah. A praying heart must be touched with the solemnity of his drawing near to the Son of God and the urgency of his need. It is wisdom (*vs. 10*) to consider David's warning of the first three poetic impressions. As Solomon said, 'Better a poor but wise youth than an old but foolish king who no longer knows how to take warning' (*Ecclesiastes 4:13*). Rulers are notorious for proud self-confidence that cannot accept anything so negative as a warning. 'The fear of the Lord is the beginning of knowledge' (*Proverbs 1:7*) even for a king. Serious impressions of sin and certain, coming judgment are necessary ingredients to saving prayer to God's Son. It must be a humble prayer.

Reverence is increased in prayer by David's reminder (in verse 12) that the One to whom we come in prayer can flare up in wrath. He has every just ground for responding in this manner toward defiant mutineers. If the holy wrath within the Son breaks out against us we will perish in the midst of our approach to him (*vs. 12*). Our hearts address the King of kings who holds in his hand an iron sceptre given him by Jehovah to destroy the likes of us.

It is our place then to announce in our prayers that we have had a change of mind. We now intend to 'serve Jehovah' (*vs. 11*). We have 'turned to God . . . to serve the living and true God' (*1 Thessalonians 1:9*). This is nothing short of thoroughgoing repentance. David is requiring a heartfelt renunciation of the ways of sin with a fully sincere intent of serving Jehovah henceforth. Tell God's Son that you have resigned from the armies of the nations and have come to enlist in the regiments of the Almighty. No longer will you spurn his law but heartily comply with it. You will 'serve the Lord', God helping you. Come with a pledge of new allegiance and a full endeavour to walk in new obedience to Jehovah. Swear off your former ways of sin with conviction in your soul that there is mercy with God for those who do so.

Then too, 'kiss the Son' upon his throne (*vs. 12*). When Samuel anointed Saul as the first king of Israel (*1 Samuel 10:1*) he kissed Saul as a symbol of homage and allegiance. Bow the knee to Jesus the Lord. Submit to him and enter the ranks of his royal subjects, ready to follow the Lamb wherever he goes or wherever he commands. You come by prayer to a great King. Worshipful submission must fill your attitude and direct your words.

'All' who thus flee to Christ for refuge will be blessed. In the midst of such a saving prayer, it is expected that refugees will experience an emotional release described by David in verse 11. Repentant rebels at the feet of Christ for the first time may well 'rejoice with trembling'. Praying sinners stand before Messiah flanked by two overwhelming realities. On the one hand is everlasting destruction from the presence of the Lord by his wrath and power, justly deserved by most obnoxious sins. At this near catastrophe of utterly perishing the sinner trembles. On the other hand there is safe refuge, forgiveness of sins, everlasting blessing and kindness from the hand of the Son of God. At this we rejoice.

A few years ago a news item reported that a painter working two hundred feet above the ground was blown off a tower (which supported high tension wires) by a gust of wind. Instinctively his arms reached out and caught a crossbar of the tower. After an agonizingly difficult climb back to earth, the workman sat in one spot for half an hour. He alternately laughed with delight that his life was spared and wept in recognition of the disaster which nearly destroyed him. In this way a sinner passing from death to life, from wrath to mercy as he stands before the throne of Christ 'rejoices with trembling'.

Some imagine that they may go to Jesus for pardon and grace without a sincere intent to serve Jehovah or a heartfelt submission to Jesus' lordship. It is a dangerous business thus to toy with him whose 'wrath can flare up in a moment' (vs. 12). David does not recommend that any seek to make Jesus Saviour without bowing to His Majesty as Lord. David has emphasized that his throne is upon a holy hill. It would not be wise for anyone to enter his presence clinging to lawless ways or intending to return to the camp of the lawbreaking nations. One must be prepared to 'serve Jehovah with fear' and to 'kiss the Son' with homage and devotion. Any other approach to the Anointed One is dangerous beyond description.

Some imagine that Messiah's offers of mercy and his delays at executing God's wrath are reasons to delay fleeing for refuge. Presumption and complacency in sin keep many from the throne of God's Son in whom is safety and deliverance. Wisdom will take warning (vs. 10). The day of the Lord will come, the day of vengeance and of the wrath of Almighty God. The day of grace will come to an end. The door at the citadel of refuge will be closed. The inscription at the palace door reads, 'Blessed are *all* who take refuge in him'. It is urgent that you go to him at once.

'Seek the Lord while he may be found; call on him while he is near. Let the wicked *forsake* his way and the evil man his thoughts. Let him *turn* to the Lord, and he will have mercy on him, and to our God, for he will freely pardon' (*Isaiah 55:6–7*). The testimony of all who have trusted in him is that Jesus is an able and willing Saviour. 'He is able to save to the uttermost those who come to God through him' (*Hebrews 7:25*). Why should you not be one of them? Why would you prefer to die? Turn, turn from your wicked ways and go to Christ following David's instructions for doing so.

Most of us who are Christians can recall our earliest approaches to God's Son in prayer. Because God's law had done its work in our consciences we went to the Lord loaded with a great weight of guilt and shame. We trembled to enter the courts of his holiness, justice and power, knowing that we were deserving of his wrath. But we had heard that enemies of heaven could have peace with God through him and that there was no other way to pardon and life.

It is the universal testimony of those who have turned to him, forsaking their sin and rebellion with grief and hatred of their foolish ways, that there has been no harshness or bitterness in the Messiah toward them. Great lovingkindness and gentleness are expressed by God's Son to all who are humbled before him. However fierce Christ may be in his dealings with the obstinate and unbowed revolutionary against his throne, 'a broken and contrite heart' he never despises (*Psalm 51:17*). All is blessing and not cursing for any who take refuge in him. Jesus Christ is meek and lowly of heart in his dealings with penitent sinners.

His grace and tenderness to us who had been outrageous felons against his own authority has set aflame in us an undying gratitude and love to the Anointed One. Christ's kind reception of us and free forgiveness for all our misconduct have made us eager to do something in return for him. We long for some way to serve him. Since he first loved us we earnestly yearn for an opportunity to show our love to him.

There are some who think that David's psalm is too heavy. These critics would delete the negative description of extraordinary lawbreaking, and the disquieting account of coming judgment. This school of thought prefers to hasten at once to the emphasis of mercy and blessing. However, such a short-cut to the grace and saving love of God is ill-advised. It is only because we have felt deeply the enormity of our sins against God and his Messiah that we realize what an infinite mercy has been shown us in the forgiveness of sins. A preview of the wrath and destruction certain to fall upon us if our insurrection continued has given us a measure of the immense blessing of pardon.

When Jesus visited the house of Simon the Pharisee (*Luke 7:36–50*), the religious host could not appreciate the outpouring of affection by a notoriously sinful woman toward the Lord Jesus. She wet Jesus' feet with her tears, wiped them with her hair, kissed his feet and poured perfume on them. Her extravagant devotion was explained by a parable which Jesus told to the perplexed Pharisee.

The lesson of our Lord's parable was that those who are forgiven much in turn greatly love the one who has forgiven them. Those who are forgiven little love little. Because this woman had understood her sinfulness to be immense, her love for Jesus who forgave her was proportionate to his gift.

It is the recognition of the heinous character of our sinful actions against God and his Son that prepares us to love him. It is the full realization that our monstrous crimes both deserved and were assigned fearful judgment that forms the foundation of gospel love in us. Christ is precious to us in proportion to how we have perceived our vileness and our danger under God's wrath. If we have received little from him, our devotion will be small. But if we have viewed ourselves and our world as did David, no service for Christ is too much to ask of us. Our love for Messiah is the greatest moving force in our beings. Our commitment to the Son of God is total. Forgiveness of sins is not a commonplace trifle. It is lovingkindness of infinite magnitude which demands everlasting love in response.

THE CORONATION

'God has made this Jesus, whom you crucified, both Lord and Christ.'

(Acts 2:36)

As a young man David became familiar with solitude because of his responsibility to shepherd Jesse's flocks. In his isolation the future hero of Israel did not fall into habits of mental laziness. Rather he exercised his mind on profound subjects. David's psalms disclose his early-formed tendency to meditate on lofty themes.

Since he is not one to allow an awesome truth to lie neglected, it does not surprise us that David mused on the stunning truth of Messiah enthroned as supreme Lord of all the earth. As we saw in Psalm 2, it had been revealed to the ancient warrior-king that Jehovah's installation of his Son upon his holy hill was *the* divine purpose which would frustrate human rebellion and *the* divine act which would dominate and give meaning to all of human history. Surely then David must further contemplate this most pivotal event of all times.

Psalm 110 suggests to us the process of the poet's mind as he deliberated upon the royal Messiah. He was keenly interested in further information regarding the coronation of the Anointed One. He wondered how supreme sovereignty for the Son of God could exist even while this world is filled with evil. He reflected upon what it would be like when the

King of kings undertook his final triumphant march
against all his and God's enemies. As David meditated,
his mind was carried along by the Holy Spirit so that he
would give to us divine answers to these most spiritual
questions.

As David's mental processes will lead us on to higher
doctrinal planes, the feelings aroused in the hymn
writer's spirit will lift us to new emotional heights. It is
obvious that the poet of long ago felt a warm glow of
reverence in beholding the majesty of the scenes about
which he wrote. His words ignite in his readers the
deep wonder of worship in the presence of the King of
kings. One can also sense the thrill of joy David felt in
the glories and triumphs of the worthy Son of God.

'Love is not self-seeking' (*1 Corinthians 13:5*). Love
does not require a personal achievement or a personal
blessing to be happy. Love is ecstatically pleased with
the honours and victories of the one who is loved. Jesus
spoke of this sort of joy on the night he was betrayed.
He said to his disciples, 'If you loved *me*, you would be
glad that *I* am going to the Father' (*John 14:28*). From
such love praise ascends in worship, giving the
worshipper a sense of delight at the exaltation and
success of our Lord Jesus Christ.

Along with the fervour of worship and the thrill of
joyful praise, Psalm 110 exudes tranquillity. The writer
of the psalm is confident that Messiah reigns. Such
certainty produces calm in the face of current affairs,
patience with the events of one's own life, satisfaction
with the Lord's management of all things, expectancy
that a glorious future is coming, confidence in the One
who sits upon the throne. His spirit is at peace. May we
too become composed and placid as we enter into what
Martin Luther called the 'crown of all the psalms'.

1 : THE POWERFUL REIGN OF CHRIST

'The Lord says to my Lord: "Sit at my right hand until I make your enemies a footstool for your feet."'

Psalm 110:1

In Old Testament times prophets were frequently called seers. Under divine inspiration these holy men would visualize future events, heavenly scenes, or spiritual realities under vivid imagery. Of course David, as a prophet, was a seer. The first verse of Psalm 110 is one of the most remarkable instances of seeing in the whole history of revelation. It is as if David had been transported forward in time 1,000 years. He alone of all Biblical writers was permitted to witness a scene in heaven and to report it to men on earth. Even New Testament apostles were not privileged to observe and publish this momentous occasion – the coronation of the Son of God.

Acts chapter one records that Jesus spent forty days with his apostles after his resurrection. Some of Jesus' very last words to them are preserved for us there. Then Acts 1:9 continues, 'After he said this, he was taken up before their very eyes, and a cloud hid him from their sight.' But what became of Jesus on the other side of the cloud? Even those who were recipients of New Testament revelation rely almost entirely on this account given by David 1,000 years earlier, when they describe what occurred to the Lord Jesus immediately after he left this earth. On the day of Pentecost Peter quotes Psalm 110:1 to express what had become of Jesus. Our Apostles' Creed summarizes all of Psalm 110 when it says that the Lord Jesus Christ 'ascended into heaven, and sitteth on the right hand of

God the Father Almighty; from thence he shall come
to judge the quick and the dead.'

John, from his visions on the Isle of Patmos,
describes for us in Revelation four and five the
grandeur of heaven where God specially dwells. He
uses the imagery both of the temple and of a throne
room. In magnificent splendour Jehovah is being constantly adored by spiritual creatures (angels and
cherubim) and by redeemed humanity (represented
by the souls of leading saints now made perfect). They
cry, 'Holy, holy, holy is the Lord God Almighty,
who was, and is, and is to come' (*Revelation 4:8*).
Falling down before him, they cast crowns before
God's throne and praise him as the creator of all.

Suddenly, as John the bystander watches, a problem is brought into focus. In the right hand of God
the Father Almighty is a scroll. The scroll represents
the great purposes of God for this earth, his eternal
decrees regarding mankind. But no one can be found
to open the scroll or execute God's plan for this
world. No mere angel or mere man is worthy to carry
out God's design for our human race. All were
perplexed by the closed and sealed scroll until there
appeared in the midst of the throne of God a Lamb
who seemed to have been slain. He is worthy to open
the scroll. The Christ, God's Lamb, is able to unfold
the great divine scheme. So the book of Revelation
proceeds with the administration of the Lamb in the
midst of God's throne.

John assists us in seeing what a glorious place it was
into which the Lord Jesus ascended. Yet even he does
not describe the initial reception which Jesus received
when he first returned to heaven. David alone is given
the assignment to reveal to us what it was like when

Messiah first arrived in God's court after his crucifixion and resurrection.

Jehovah spoke from his throne of universal and absolute dominion to his Son returning from the earthly mission on which he had sent him. This Lamb of God had recently heard the multitudes shout, 'Crucify him! Away with this man! We have no king but Caesar! His blood be upon us and upon our children!' Cruel and violent jokes were played on him, followed by hilarious laughter. They pierced his hands and his feet. What would the Father say, the Father who had filled Messiah's cup with these bitter dregs of torment? Pilate and the Gentiles only did to Jesus what the Father had decided beforehand should happen (*Acts 4:28*). What now would he say in this highly dramatic moment of reunion?

As Jesus the Christ re-entered the throne-room-temple of heaven, the seat of heavenly glory shook with the anthems of church elders and cherubim. 'Worthy is the Lamb, who was slain, to receive power and wealth and wisdom and strength and honour and glory and praise!' (*Revelation 5:12*). But above the thundering chorus of praise, the risen Saviour heard the words of Jehovah, 'Sit at my right hand until I make your enemies a footstool for your feet.'

From the lowest imaginable position as the sin bearer of his people, who had been despised and rejected by men and bruised by divine justice, Jesus returned to the Father to be given a position of supreme dignity and dominion. It was the Father himself who seated Messiah upon the throne.

Some Bible teachers have taught that Jesus Christ is a figure to be pitied. They teach that Jesus entered the earth to become a king. He offered his rule to the Jews, but they rejected him. Consequently, they depict Jesus as having left this earth in weakness and defeat. He is viewed as an exile in heaven, driven off the earth by the hatred of men. They suggest that he will one day return to earth, then to take up the Jewish throne he had previously sought. No such ideas about Jesus 'becoming' Lord could be more unbiblical or more distant from the truth.

Our Saviour never intended that *men* should crown him as a king. His becoming Lord was never conditioned upon choices of the human will. Jesus had no intention of being made a king by popular selection. He sought to stifle his spreading popularity by instructing his disciples and those whom he miraculously healed not to tell anyone who he was.

On one occasion, after the miracle of feeding the 5,000, we are told, 'Jesus, knowing that they intended to come and make him king by force, withdrew again to a mountain by himself' (*John 6:15*). Had our Master been seeking rule by popular acclaim, it was quite within reach on that day. Pharisees were seeking to kill him just because Jesus' influence upon the people was so great that their leadership was threatened. But the Son of God was not looking for any man to make him Lord. His aim was to receive a crown which no human mandate could give him.

How well the Messiah understood the only possible source for investiture with the kingly office he sought! On the night of his betrayal Christ prayed, 'And now Father, glorify me in your presence with the glory I had with you before the world began' (*John 17:5*). Shortly after the crucifixion, the Son of God incarnate was taken into the glorious presence of the Father, there to have Jehovah himself place the diadem upon his head. Then he sat upon the throne he asked to occupy, not a Jewish seat of power in Palestine, but the very throne of God Almighty which is over all.

'*God* exalted him to the highest place' (*Philippians 2:9*). '*God* has made this Jesus, whom you crucified, both Lord and Christ' (*Acts 2:36*). 'The *Lord* [Jehovah] says unto my Lord: "Sit at my right hand"' (*Psalm 110:1*). It is not up to you whether or not Jesus will be your Lord. It never was a matter for human decision individually or collectively. God settled that matter before ever you were born. It is the prerogative of the Most High to set up and cast down even human rulers. But no man has ever been used as even a secondary cause of installing anyone on God's throne.

The true and living God has placed upon his throne of infinite sovereignty the very One whom men rejected at Calvary. Jesus has been given absolute power over all the human race, bodies and souls. It is not the business of preachers to beg people to make Jesus Lord, as if his kingdom were in doubt. Preaching the gospel is to proclaim that by irreversible decree God has placed Jesus in full command of our world. One divine vote overrides all the ballots cast by Jews and Gentiles to the contrary. It is the preacher's duty to make you aware that you exist under the government of Jesus whom God has placed upon the throne.

We do beseech all men to come to terms with the supreme authority of Christ. Since Jehovah has given Jesus complete jurisdiction over your life, over all circumstances and events of the world you live in, and over your destiny, it is urgent that you bow to him as Lord, confess allegiance to him, and submit to his commands as the rule of your life. No stubborn refusal can overthrow his regency. No resistance can change the fact of his lordship. Rebellion can bring only everlasting and unpleasant consequences of his power to the obstinate. 'God exalted him . . . so that at the name of Jesus every knee should bow, in heaven and on earth and under the earth, and every tongue confess that Jesus Christ is Lord, to the glory of God the Father' (*Philippians 2:10,11*). He is your Sovereign either to save or to destroy.

Had Jesus received his ordination from men, how fleeting his power would have been. John tells us that 'many people saw the miraculous signs he was doing and believed in his name. But Jesus would not entrust himself to them, for he knew all men' (*John 2:23,24*). He was fully aware of the fickleness and unreliability of fallen man. Human choice would be shifting sand upon which to build an empire. Our Lord's head was not even turned by the chorus of 'Hosanna to the Son of David' at his 'triumphal' entry to Jerusalem.

As he was approaching Jerusalem he told a parable about himself. 'A man of noble birth' was about to go to a distant country to be appointed as king. The citizens of the land he would rule were about to send a message to the monarch who was about to crown him. The message would read, 'We don't want this man to be our king' (*Luke 19:11–27*). He knew that the very voices soon to cry, 'Blessed is the king who comes in the name of the Lord' would shortly thereafter cry, 'Crucify him!' Messiah would patiently wait for the Father to make him King.

Jehovah's invitation to 'sit' does not suggest any inactivity or rest. Jesus was not told to sit in order to wait for another hour when he would reign. When a judge takes his seat, the court is in session and the work of justice proceeds. When a king sits upon a throne, he does so to attend to the affairs of state. Messiah was seated upon a throne to manage everything in heaven and earth which has any relevance to humanity and its world. 'He's got the whole world in his hands', goes a negro spiritual. He sits to direct all matters great and small, complex and simple upon the earth.

The place assigned by the Father for this magnificent royal administration is 'at my right hand'. It is elevation to the highest possible honour. At God's right hand is the seat of utmost esteem. Publicly seating his Son upon his right side is the most evident expression of his own approval of his Son's work. Whatever men may think of Christ or say of him, the Father has paid the Son his supreme compliment. Imagine those who mocked Jesus, who rejected the claims of Jesus and who crucified Jesus entering God's throne room to find our Saviour in the position of pre-eminent distinction. God has rewarded the Son with praise. The mouths of men must be stopped.

In addition, the right arm is a symbol of strength. Jesus, fresh from his redemptive work, is not to be seated next to the Father momentarily. The Son is permanently installed upon the Father's right hand to share all of his authority and to administer his will. At Jehovah's right hand, the ensign of royal might, Christ will participate in the totality of divine power and dominion. This is power that need only speak and it is done, need only command and it stands fast.

Consider also the influence of our Lord's position. No issue is deliberated by the Father without the Son's presence to express his counsel and wishes. Any concern of Jesus may be addressed immediately to the Almighty, for he has continual access. Messiah will not be excluded from any process of government in heaven. He is God's 'right hand man' and will not be bypassed in any divine transactions. He is on the throne with the Father as the One through whom all affairs in heaven and upon earth will be managed. He is directly involved in all decision-making.

We should not think that the Lord seated Christ on a throne next to but separate from his own. To envision two thrones side by side would be a mistake. It is common for rulers of the East to have seats that are as wide as our sofas. Honoured dignitaries are invited to sit with the ruler on his throne (see Jesus' promise to his saints in Revelation 3:21). There is but one throne in heaven. Jesus Christ shares it with Jehovah, sitting at his right hand of power, glory and influence.

Jehovah's first words to his returning Suffering Servant designate the longevity and the culmination of Messiah's session at his right hand: 'until I make your enemies a footstool for your feet.' It is the stated intention of the Lord of heaven and earth personally to subjugate to Christ everyone who is Messiah's enemy. These words, spoken at his coronation, bring to us memories of Joshua's treatment of the five Amorite kings at the conquest of Canaan. When the five rulers were captured, Joshua called all his army commanders to put their feet on the necks of the vanquished before they were slain. This symbol of complete victory over their foes greatly encouraged Israel's military leaders for future battles (*Joshua 10:22–26*). If all the Anointed One's enemies are put under his feet, then none will be left to topple his throne. His reign must and will endure forever.

From this first greeting given to Christ after his earthly mission we still need to consider the greatness of Jesus' person. Pharisees were constantly putting loaded questions to Jesus. They were hoping to catch him in a public blunder to discredit him and accuse him of false teaching. Near the end of his ministry, Jesus of Nazareth turned the tables on them. He asked a question of the Pharisees, 'What do you think about the Christ? Whose son is he?' (*Matthew 22:42*). These proud theologians answered, accurately but inadequately, 'The Son of David.' Then the great Teacher put them to silence with these words, 'How is it then that David, speaking by the Spirit, calls him "Lord"? For he says, the Lord said to *my* Lord: Sit at my right hand until I put your enemies under your feet. If then David calls him "Lord", how can he be his son?'

David, the writer of Psalm 110 is one of the most venerable saints of all the ages. He was a mighty man of faith who subdued Israel's enemies, beginning with the defeat of Goliath. Through a lifetime of courage he brought peace and prosperity to God's people. He was a holy man who knew God. His gift of prophecy has produced the psalms which continue to this day as the chief prayerbook of the Church.

Yet when David spoke of Messiah to come, he did not refer to him as 'my son' or 'my descendant'. The exalted dignity of Christ's person demanded more than that. With bowed knee and with fear in his heart, the greatest king of ancient Israel called him '*my* Lord'. Jesus 'was a descendant of David as to his human nature' (*Romans 1:3*). But Jesus was also the Son of God (*of divine nature*) so that even the ancestors of his humanity bowed down to worship him as Lord.

There is much of modern religion and modern religious literature that has become flippant. Some speak to Jesus and about Jesus with the same casual, back-slapping familiarity that they would use in talking with a peer. 'Hey, Jesus', and 'Good morning, Jesus', and 'Let's give Christ a hand' (as if he were a performing artist). We hear of 'getting high on Jesus' and so forth.

David realized that a commoner does not address the dread majesty of a powerful sovereign with presumption and impertinence. Jesus Christ is the eternal Son of God, seated at the right hand of the Majesty on high with everlasting, universal dominion over all men. He is Master of the Universe and the final Judge of mankind. The apostle John on the Isle of Patmos had a vision of the exalted Christ, and he reports, 'When I saw him, I fell at his feet as though dead' (*Revelation 1:17*). When Thomas realized that he was in the company of the resurrected Christ, he cried, 'My Lord and my God' (*John 20:28*). When Jesus healed a blind man and afterward instructed the poor man that he who had healed him was the Son of God, 'The man said, "Lord, I believe," and he worshipped him' (*John 9:38*). David, too, called him, 'my Lord'.

Anyone who has caught a glimpse of the heavenly splendour and sovereign might of Christ would do well to imitate the saints of ages past. It is only appropriate to worship him with deep reverence. You may pour out great love in recognition of your personal relationship with him. He is your Lord. You are his and he is yours. However, you are not pals. He is Lord and Master. You are servant and disciple. He is infinitely above you in the scale of being. His throne holds sway over you for your present life and for assigning your eternal reward. A king is to be honoured, confessed, obeyed, and worshipped.

Such humble gestures of adoration are the responses

required in our gospel. 'If you confess with your mouth, "Jesus is Lord," and believe in your heart that God raised him from the dead, you will be saved' (*Romans 10:9*).

What joy does this scene revealed by David bring to all who trust in Jesus Christ! The God of heaven has set up a kingdom that will never be destroyed. It will crush all other kingdoms and bring them to an end, but this kingdom will endure forever (*Daniel 2:44*). 'The Lord reigns, let the earth be glad; let distant shores rejoice . . . Fire goes before him and consumes his foes on every side . . . The mountains melt like wax before the Lord, before the Lord of all the earth . . . all peoples see his glory . . . For you, O Lord, are the Most High over all the earth . . . Rejoice in the Lord and praise his holy name' (*Psalm 97*). 'Rejoice *in the Lord* always' (*Philippians 4:4*).

Christ sits upon the throne of God with Jehovah's pledge that all things will be put under his feet. Christ reigns as a true man as well as true God. In him we too are heirs of heavenly glory and power. With Jesus God has freely given to us all things.

When frustration and fear enter our hearts, we need but to look unto Jesus who is guiding the affairs of our time. He is enthroned at God's right hand. He is in session. He has the whole world in his hands. He is directing all things for the good of his people the Church, for the demolition of sin, death, ungodliness and the devil. We can pillow our heads safely, having been told of the coronation of the Son of God. 'The Lord is my salvation – whom shall I fear? The Lord is the stronghold of my life – of whom shall I be afraid?' (*Psalm 27:1*). With his eminent position of power, he 'is able to keep you from falling and to present you before his glorious presence without fault and with great joy' (*Jude 24*). Every gospel promise and gospel comfort rests upon the throne of Christ. Who would exchange the present, triumphant, heavenly reign of Jesus Christ for a temporary, future Jewish throne granted by the will of mere men?

2: THE SPIRITUAL REIGN OF CHRIST

'*The Lord will extend your mighty sceptre from Zion; you will rule in the midst of your enemies. Your troops will be willing on your day of battle. Arrayed in holy majesty, from the womb of the dawn you will receive the dew of your youth.*'

Psalm 110: 2–3.

It is very moving to describe in majestic terms the divine power with which Jesus has been invested as King at Jehovah's right hand. However, we find it very difficult to identify the kingdom over which Messiah reigns at present. We stand in awe at descriptions of the future display of his matchless might, when every enemy shall be vanquished, when his foot rests upon the necks of all his foes, when there shall be such revelation of his greatness that every knee shall be compelled to bow. That is dominion that we understand and readily identify.

But we are living in a world in which Jesus' enemies are flourishing and aggressive. Atheistic humanism is vigorous and triumphant over vast regions of the earth. So too do false religions hold large regions of our world in their effective grip. Everywhere in the 'Christian' West there is a floodtide of immorality, false religion, and utter unbelief. The Church herself is persecuted from without and betrayed into the hands of heretical theology from within. This occurs the world round. Where is the territory of this King?

One can easily understand why so many doubt that Christ is yet a King. Even the pious John the Baptist sent to ask Jesus if he was the promised One or if he and his followers should look for another. It was rather difficult to see Jesus' sphere of dominion. John had expected mighty displays of kingly conquest. Pilate asked him in rather puzzled tones, 'Are you a king, then?' (*John 18:37*). Where was his royal realm? The people denied his authority; he had no army, no palace, no treasury, no visible government. No wonder the hearts of some echo this perplexity by saying, 'Well, the reign of Christ has not yet begun, but it will come some day.'

A few saw glimmers of kingly power when Jesus commanded winds and waves to obey him, or when he cast out devils, or when he raised the dead, or when he was resurrected. They saw miracles and believed that he was then a King. Anticipating our day when his own earthly presence and miracle working would cease, Jesus said, 'Blessed are those who have not seen and yet have believed' (*John 20:29*).

There is something exceedingly mysterious about the present phase of the governance of the Son of God. It is expressed to him in verse 2 in these words, 'You will rule in the midst of your enemies.' Never before has there been a kingdom like this! Rulers make boundaries. Enemies are forcefully thrust outside the frontiers of their provinces. Power is defined by the extent to which a king's borders are free from rivals. But Messiah will reign in the midst of his enemies' presence! In the place where opponents rage against him with all of their most malicious activities, there will Messiah's kingdom be established and dominant.

At its present stage the kingdom of Messiah is invisible to most eyes. Only the spiritually alert can detect the mighty reins which he holds, controlling every event upon the earth. Judging from the anxiety and discouragement found in the hearts of those who love Jesus and confess that he is Lord, his power must be quite difficult to discern indeed. His rule is emphatically spiritual. While the Anointed One sits in heaven in the midst of his friends and admirers, he superintends the earth in the midst of his enemies.

Our Lord's session at God's right hand has been assigned spiritual objectives for the earth. During this era of mighty power, Messiah is gathering a people to himself, a volunteer army. 'Your people [or troops] will be willing [or free-will offerings] in the day of your power' (*vs. 3*). Loyalists to King Jesus are a holy people, dedicated to moral righteousness: 'Arrayed in holy majesty' (*vs. 3*). As at the dawning of the day dew gathers with the freshness of youth and with countless droplets, so are the followers of the King of glory. 'From the womb of the dawn you will receive the dew of your youth.'

Messiah has entered the very camp of the enemy. From the veritable ranks of the armies of his hostile foes the Son of God recruits his own forces. Not a few are enrolled in his ranks from the very gates of Hell. They are as numerous as the drops of dew at daybreak. They come from every nation, tribe and people. Each follower of the Lamb once shared the hatred of Messiah's person and rule, once eagerly rebelled against his law and throne. But now they are arrayed in shining purity, like the glistening dew of the early day. Such is the greatness of Messiah's might that none has been forced into service. The army of Christ has never conscripted its troops. Each one has been mysteriously, secretly made willing in the depths of his being.

David's Lord has not immediately exterminated his enemies, because countless of them must be enrolled in the army of the Son of God. A great host that no man can number will voluntarily leave the militia of Jesus' enemies and, with youthful enthusiasm, enlist in the regiments of Messiah. They will come from the midst of universities which are most vehement and most skilled in sceptical arguing against the kingdom of God. Many will throw off the most powerful allurements in the midst of sinful pleasures. Multitudes will emerge from the midst of the mightiest satanic influences to enter their names in the register of the saints. The chief of sinners will become Jesus' troops in this age.

Saul of Tarsus is but one example of those who hated the name of Jesus. Breathing out threatenings, this passionate opponent of the cause of Christ was marching against any who used Jesus' name. Armed with official permission to imprison Christians and filled with fanatical hatred of the Church, Saul proceeded to Damascus. But suddenly his mind and heart were transformed. Made willing under the power of Christ he cries, 'What shall I do, Lord?' Soon he who sought to crush the Church was preaching Christ in the synagogues. In the midst of his enemies Jesus is Lord, taking men captive by an astonishing power which turns them into willing subjects. They present their bodies as living sacrifices and think it reasonable service! His power has made them willing.

There is a glory to be seen in the final overthrow of obstinate enemies of the Son of God. But, oh, that spiritual eyes could behold the splendour and majesty in the present reign of Jesus Christ. By effectual calling, devoted mutineers against his throne become bowed and loving subjects. By the regeneration of his mighty Spirit, foul sinners are 'arrayed in holy majesty'. Stubborn wills are bent to yielded compliance by his infinite strength and mysterious working.

As our Lord's session upon the throne of the Almighty is exercised for spiritual goals, so in his session he uses spiritual means. 'The Lord will extend your mighty sceptre [or rod] from Zion' (*vs. 2*). What Christ accomplishes in the midst of his enemies he achieves through his Church. His mighty, transforming power which makes enemies willing to serve as his troops flows through the conduit of his Church.

How weak and insignificant the Church may appear. She is crushed and opposed by world governments. She is turned aside from her mission by false prophets. She is weakened and betrayed into enemy hands by the pleasures and possessions of a depraved world. Yet the sceptre of Sovereign Messiah extends from holy Zion to all the regions of his enemies. It is the Church of Christ which storms the gates of Hell to swell the ranks of God's Son.

When Paul the apostle and his few assistants made a visit to Corinth, they had entered sin city. Corinth was a centre of heathen power, the very political force that had crucified Jesus. Corinth was a centre of idolatrous religion. Corinth exuded all the possible corruptions of wealth, drunkenness, sex for hire (male or female). Furthermore, the Jewish synagogue at Corinth opposed Paul and became abusive. What could a few missionaries do in the very seat of pagan vice? One night Jesus spoke to Paul and said, 'Do not be afraid; keep on speaking . . . I am with you . . . I have many people in this city' (*Acts 18:9–10*). The Church was the

[65]

conduit of Messianic power to snatch brands from the fire, to turn great sinners to repentance, to recruit the army of the King of kings.

Too often the Church imagines that her task is to stake out a region and Christianize it. If only we could build a fully consistent Christian society and utterly stamp out the powers of darkness, we think. By laws or military conquest or by retreat from the world we will build Christian enclaves. That will demonstrate the power of Christ, it is thought. But that is not Christ's plan for the Church. Believers are the light of the world. Lights are placed in darkness. The Church is the extension of Messiah's rod into the camp of the enemy. His people are sent out as sheep in the midst of wolves.

In this era, the Church must expect to be in close contact with the enemies of God's Son so that through his people his mighty power may seize upon some of the enemy and win them to Christ. Through vain imaginings that she must be presently triumphant in a visible, political and territorial sense, the Church has too often abandoned her majestic and mighty work. She has failed even to attempt to penetrate the strongholds of Christ's enemies. And she has exchanged the 'mighty sceptre' of Christ for earthly weapons. At times the Church has attempted to impose her will upon men with the sword of government. How sad to observe evangelicals in America being so excited about employing the Church's energies in political activism.

Paul rightly commented, 'Though we live in the world, we do not wage war as the world does. The weapons we fight with are not the weapons of the world. On the contrary they have divine power to demolish strongholds' (2 *Corinthians* 10:3,4). The Church's weapons are spiritual: prayer, preaching

God's Word and an indwelling Holy Spirit. Never has the Church done well on battlefields or in halls of government. She only demolishes when she attacks strongholds with prayer and preaching God's Word and doing both while filled with the Holy Spirit.

David must have sensed that the spiritual phase of Jesus' reign over the earth would be a dramatic change from the era in which he was living. Reigning in the midst of enemies was a foreign concept to the Mosaic covenant. Through Moses a 'dividing wall of hostility' (*Ephesians 2:14*) had been erected between Jew and Gentile. God's people lived within a society which excluded the Lord's fiercest enemies. Heathen were kept at a great distance when Israel's armies were successful. While this policy protected the saints, it effectively shut the Gentiles out of the grace of God. God's enemies were held at a distance from his truth and from the means of grace.

When Christ 'destroyed the barrier' (*Ephesians 2:14*) between Jew and Gentile, the Mosaic economy was effectively ended; for it established an external, territorial kingdom. The Church was sent *into* all the world to disciple the nations to Messiah. We are not to wrestle against flesh and blood but against spiritual forces of evil in the heavenly realms (*Ephesians 6:12*). Our wrestling is to loosen the grip of these dark spiritual powers upon the souls of perishing sinners. How sad when the Church's energies are turned away from the work of evangelism back into the business of statecraft. It is a denial of the glory of Messiah's spiritual reign as well as a retreat to Mosaic strategy.

Cities of the western world are coming under deeper darkness. They are increasingly the citadels of ungodly forces. Nations lie under the grip of materialism and other false ideologies. All are in desperate need of a spiritual Church using spiritual weapons to fight a spiritual war, under the spiritual reign of Christ. If the Lord will arise in his might from heaven, it will be through Zion. When he does, 'his troops will be willing in the day of his power'. It is their glory and joy to be a little band in the midst of Christ's enemies. For then it will appear that divine power attends them in their spiritual battle. Their numbers must increase as Jesus' mighty sceptre is extended.

How foolish it is to attempt to compel the unwilling to submit to Christ. They only belong to the Lord who are willing in the day of his power. Deborah sang of the great victory over Canaanite kings in these words, 'When the people willingly offer themselves – praise the Lord! . . . the mountains quaked before the Lord' (*Judges 5:2ff*). David offered himself to fight Goliath, driven by a zeal for the glory of the living God. Isaiah cried, 'Here am I. Send me' (*Isaiah 6:8*). There is no coercion in Christ's kingdom. 'I delight to do thy will, O my God . . . your law is within my heart' (*Psalm 40:8*) is the universal watchword of his troops. His people are zealous to do good works (*Titus 2:14*).

What power is being exercised by the Son of God from the right hand of the Father in our day! Power that can make a hateful, stubborn sinner into a loving, volunteer servant is magnificent. His might accomplishes such fundamental transformation of character so gently that sinners come most freely, having been made willing by his grace. It is a new creation of a fallen human soul. It is resurrection from the dead for man's spirit. It is a new birth for the human heart. It is the most remarkable power in all the world for its irresistible force and its beautiful and kind results. The excellency of this might is obviously from God. How can the Church ever be turned from the gospel to other things? 'It is the power of God unto salvation' (*Romans 1:16*). In the gospel Jesus' mighty sceptre is extended from Zion making men willing. It is the day of his power. This surpasses in majesty the work of miracles in the material realm. Beside it nuclear wars pale into insignificance and political empires appear weak. Christ rules in the midst of enemies!

3: THE PRIESTLY REIGN OF CHRIST

'*The Lord has sworn and will not change his mind: "You are a priest forever, in the order of Melchizedek."*'

Psalm 110:4

Prophets of old spoke the very words of God. Consequently they did not fully comprehend the messages they delivered. Peter (*1 Peter 1:10–12*) indicated that the very men who recorded divine revelation 'searched intently and with the greatest care' to understand what their own prophecies meant. I wonder if David was not startled by the fourth verse of his own Psalm 110. It could well have provoked questions for his personal meditations.

Any Hebrew living under the system of Moses would have been jolted by these words. No one of the tribe of Judah had ever been made a priest. No one of the tribe of Levi had served as king. Priestly and kingly functions were never performed by the same individual. Many years after this hymn was composed, Uzziah, the king of Judah, attempted to burn incense to the Lord at the temple. Azariah, an 80 year old priest, told the king that it was not right for him to perform priestly duties (2 *Chronicles 26: 16–21*). When the monarch insisted on doing a priestly act, Jehovah struck Uzziah with leprosy.

David's words predict a coming new covenant, a very different arrangement from that of Moses. The same Messiah whom Jehovah made Lord of all is invested with priesthood by divine oath. Not only will one individual be both priest and King, but this priest had his office confirmed by Jehovah's solemn vow. No other priest had ever received office attended with God's oath! This was to be a priesthood of infinitely higher dignity than that of Aaron. Messiah would be priest of a much better covenant. The Son of God serves in the priestly clan of a shadowy figure of Abraham's time, Melchizedek, the only other person ever to be both priest and king.

Since we are ignorant, weak and helpless we stand in need of a king. Christ Jesus is Lord to govern all our affairs with wisdom and power. We look to him on Jehovah's throne both to direct us with his judicious commandments and to defend us by his mighty sceptre. In his strength we will be protected from the harm our enemies intend against us. Messiah will sovereignly destroy all his and our foes in due time. Till then his administration of this world will frustrate their purposes against us. How we praise God that the risen Christ has been made Lord.

In addition to our ignorance, weakness and helplessness, we are guilty sinners. As condemned violators of God's holy law we stand in need of a priest. A priest must offer sacrifices for his client, to satisfy the demands of divine justice against his offences. With an appropriate ransom, the priest must then enter the presence of the Judge of all the earth to intercede on behalf of the sinner he represents. After making successful entreaties for the guilty, the priest then emerges from his pleadings before God's throne to pronounce benediction upon those whom he has served. Forgiveness of sins, reconciliation with God, release from the curse, removal of wrath are all announced by the efficient priest. And if he is a good priest, the sacrifice, intercession and benediction are conducted with a deep sense of compassion for the guilty sinner.

David, through the Spirit, foresaw that his Lord at Jehovah's right hand is the only priest worthy of a sinner's trust. The Son of God is the only priest who can supply suitable provision for all the urgent necessities of our case. We have 'sinned and fall short of the glory of God' (*Romans 3:23*). 'The wages of sin is death' (*Romans 6:23*). We are by our sinful nature the objects of divine wrath (*Ephesians 2:3*). What a relief for the guilty conscience to secure for himself 'an advocate with the Father, Jesus Christ, the Righteous One' (*1 John 2:1*).

Those who realize that they are guilty of malicious lawbreaking and of treason against the Almighty should put their case into the hands of the One at God's right hand. This is done by placing complete confidence in Jesus' priestly skills and by submission to his kingly authority. It is not possible to approach Jesus asking him to be your priest unless you are ready to bow to him as Lord; for the priest sits on God's throne! Of course a sinner requests the King to be his priest by heartfelt prayer.

What extensive encouragements our text gives to condemned sinners to trust in the Messiah-Priest! Jehovah himself has sworn that his Son is a duly qualified priest. No other person in heaven or on earth has ever had it confirmed by an oath of God that his priesthood is recognized and acceptable in the throne room of the Most High. The Living God has certified in sworn testimony that Jesus' priestly activities are sanctioned by his infinite authority. If ever Jesus takes upon himself to mediate your dispute with the Holy One, there will be no question that his credentials to act as priest are in order. However desperate your condition as sinner, however unfavourable your case seems, this Advocate Jesus Christ will be honourably received at court when he represents you.

Other priests, those of the clan of Aaron, could only serve as authorized agents for sinners over a brief time. Being mortal men their service to sinners was terminated by death. In contrast this Lord of David was declared by Jehovah to be a priest 'forever'. His ministrations as priest rest upon the platform of an indestructible life! Jesus rose from the dead, ascended into heaven and sits at God's right hand forevermore. 'There have been many of those priests, since death prevented them from continuing in office; but because Jesus lives forever, he has a permanent priesthood. Therefore he is able to save completely those who come to God through him, because he always lives to intercede for them' (*Hebrews 7:23–25*).

If you cast yourself upon Christ, you will never need any other priest. In serious and complex cases litigation can be prolonged. He alone can carry our trial before God through to completion. Even if we go down to the grave, he will continue at God's right hand to plead our cause. His everlasting function as priest will guarantee that he will stand by our side in the day of judgment. He alone can pronounce and bring to pass eternal benedictions. His blessings upon his people will never end.

A further encouragement to trust him arises from the place of his priestly ventures. All other priests perform their ministries upon the earth. Moses built a tabernacle patterned after the dwelling place of God. Levitical priests served sinners in a copy and shadow of heaven. But the Son of God, after he had offered up a sacrifice for our sins, entered into the real Holy of Holies. He 'sat down at the right hand of the throne of the Majesty in heaven' (*Hebrews 8:1*). He ever lives in the actual sanctuary.

At God's right hand is the position of ultimate favour. The Almighty is ever inclined to hear the petitions of the Son at his right hand. In his own solemn Word he has promised to give attention to the sacrifice and intercession of this priest. The benefits of Christ's precious blood are mentioned in the right ear of God for every sinner this priest represents. Nail-prints in his hands and feet are kept before the immediate presence of Almighty God for all the clients of this priest. The evidence of the sacrifice and the official prayers of the priest are where Christ is – forever on God's throne. Jesus does not call from afar. From the Father's bosom, he whispers in the ear of the Father on behalf of his sheep.

Is there any wonder that our Lord Jesus declared, 'I am *the* way and *the* truth and *the* life. No one comes to the Father except through me.' No other sacrifice will do but the one which he offered. No other intercession can succeed but his. 'Salvation is found in no one else, for there is no other name under heaven given to men by which we *must* be saved' (*Acts 4:12*). There is none other Lamb for sacrifice. There is none other priest who can sit upon God's throne, there speaking for us, and continue forever to represent us in our guilt. He alone can bring peace and pardon.

Who would not seek for the aid of this priest after the order of Melchizedek? It could only be those who fail to recognize that an emergency of guilt and condemnation and wrath has overtaken them. For those alarmed by the plight brought on by their evil rebellion, the announcement of Messiah's priesthood is the best of news.

4: THE JUDICIAL REIGN OF CHRIST

'The Lord is at your right hand; he will crush kings on the day of his wrath. He will judge the nations, heaping up the dead and crushing the rulers of the whole earth. He will drink from a brook beside the way; therefore he will lift up his head.'

Psalm 110: 5–7

David's concluding remarks in this psalm celebrate Messiah's final assault upon the enemies of his kingdom. This scene is most sanguine. An ancient warrior-poet employs imagery imprinted on his mind by familiar experiences of lusty hand-to-hand combat. Only one who has shared the virile bravery of having vanquished adversaries by force of arms could memorialize the last triumph of the Son of God.

It seems as though David is addressing Jehovah as he reflects on Messiah's campaign on the last day. 'The Lord is at your right hand; he will crush kings' (*see vs. 5*). The last storming of all the strongholds of darkness is being delayed as the Anointed One spoils their kingdoms with a spiritual power exercised in their very midst. With gracious might the King-Priest is receiving the dew of his youth. Yet when the day of grace ends, Messiah will arise from his throne dressed as a man of war to invade this earth. The King at God's right hand will bring this world's history to a conclusion with a decisive defeat of all terrorists against his realm.

There is to be a day of fury for the Son of God. David speaks in verse five of 'the day of his wrath' ('*The Lord is at your right hand; he will crush kings on the day of his wrath*'). Thrilling excitement rises in an experienced soldier at the sight of heroic battle. David speaks with ecstasy as he views by revelation the consummate prowess of the Mighty Victor–Messiah in his ultimate overthrow of all his antagonists.

'He will crush kings on the day of his wrath. He will judge the nations, heaping up the dead and crushing the rulers of the whole earth' (*vss. 5–6*). From the lips of one man of valour come words of admiration and acclaim for the greatest of all heroes. Christ Jesus is 'the Lion of the tribe of Judah' (*Revelation 5:5*).

David's military career began on the day he put to flight the entire army of the Philistines by killing their champion, Goliath. Abner ushered David into the presence of Saul while the youth still held the gory head of the giant. At that moment 'Jonathan became one in spirit with David and he loved him as himself' (*1 Samuel 18:1*). Israelite girls could sing, 'David has slain his tens of thousands' (*1 Samuel 18:7*) in tribute, but only Jonathan could fully appreciate David's battlefield triumph; for Jonathan too had put to flight an entire army of the Philistines with none to assist him but his armour bearer (*1 Samuel 14*).

These were days of mighty exploits and feats of courage. One of David's men killed eight hundred opponents with his spear in one encounter. Another stood his ground while defending against a Philistine attack when all the rest of the Israelite forces retreated. He struck down great heaps of enemy soldiers with his sword until his hand froze to his weapon with fatigue (*2 Samuel 23:8ff*). How the band of troopers loved to retell these sturdy acts of valour! How they loved one another for these herculean achievements on the battlefield! Especially was this true when their fellow-heroes were moved to manly acts by a zeal for the Lord of Hosts.

By revelation David saw Messiah go to war on the last day of the history of this earth. For all his experience with fighting men, never had he seen anything to approach the manly deeds of Messiah, the tireless bravery of the Son of God. At once he was one in spirit with the One at God's right hand. He loved him as himself. He was compelled to eulogize the feats of his last conquest. He must lead the shouts of acclaim! It is the lusty cheer of one great warrior overwhelmed by another's legendary might and stamina.

Single-handedly Messiah crushes kings. In David's day shrewd and victorious soldiers sat upon thrones. Christ will overthrow great world powers. He engages the kings of the whole earth and slays the nations, heaping up their dead. He fights and overcomes the mighty.

John's Revelation takes up this impassioned admiration of the Son of God and his exploits on the last day: 'I saw heaven standing open and there before me was a white horse, whose rider is called Faithful and True. With justice he judges and makes war. His eyes are like blazing fire, and on his head are many crowns. He has a name written on him that no one knows but he himself. He is dressed in a robe dipped in blood, and his name is the Word of God. The armies of heaven were following him, riding on white horses and dressed in fine linen, white and clean. Out of his mouth comes a sharp sword with which to strike down the nations. "He will rule them with an iron sceptre." He treads the wine press of the fury of the wrath of God Almighty. On his robe and on his thigh he has this name written: KING OF KINGS AND LORD OF LORDS. And I saw an angel standing in the sun, who cried in a loud voice to all the birds flying in midair, "Come, gather together for the great supper of God, so that you may eat the flesh of kings, generals, and mighty men, of horses and their riders, and the flesh of all people, free and slave, small and great." Then I saw the beast and the kings of the earth and their armies gathered together to make war against the rider on the horse and his army. But the beast was captured, and with him the false prophet who had performed the miraculous signs on his behalf. With these signs he had deluded those who had received the mark of the beast and worshiped his image. The two of them were thrown alive into the fiery lake of burning sulphur. The rest of them were killed with the sword that came out of the mouth of the rider on the horse, and all the birds gorged themselves on their flesh' (*Revelation 19:11–21*).

This description of birds of prey gorging themselves with the enemies of God's Son is reminiscent of the discussion between Goliath and David. 'The Philistine cursed David by his gods. "Come here," he said, "and I'll give your flesh to the birds of the air and the beasts of the field!"' (*1 Samuel 17:43,44*). Not to be outdone in courage when facing his enemy, 'David said to the

Philistine, "You come against me with sword and spear and javelin, but I come against you in the name of the Lord Almighty, the God of the armies of Israel, whom you have defied. This day the Lord will hand you over to me, and I'll strike you down and cut off your head. Today I will give the carcasses of the Philistine army to the birds of the air and the beasts of the earth, and the whole world will know that there is a God in Israel"' (*1 Samuel 17:45,46*).

A conquering general would watch buzzards swarm over the carrion of vanquished foes. It was an awesome scene confirming to all nearby that he was a mighty victor. The devastation to be brought by the final march of the Son of God will be unequalled by the bloodiest wars of human history. As the Lord Jesus rides into the last conflict, an angel standing in the sun invites all the birds of prey to gather for the ultimate conquest.

Such is the magnitude of the victory of Messiah at his second coming, that all his people are victors with him. This in fact will be the war to end all wars. Justice will be done to all who pierced him at his first coming. Those who killed apostles and martyrs will be slain. Persecutors of the people of God will be forever destroyed. 'He will pay back trouble to those who trouble you, and give relief to you who are troubled . . . when the Lord Jesus is revealed from heaven in blazing fire . . . ' (*2 Thessalonians 1:6,7*). His bombardment of the rulers of the whole earth is salvation and victory for all members of his kingdom.

Some can recall their homes, nations, freedoms and ways of life having been under siege by sinister opponents. With what joy and gratitude did they hear of assailants successfully overthrown by their armies. With what exultant cheers did they greet their returning, conquering heroes. All the world loved to hear of a Hitler crushed, of an evil empire heaped up with dead. So too will all God's people join David in extolling our mighty Lord. 'Hallelujah! Salvation and glory and power belong to our God, for true and just are his judgments. He has condemned the great prostitute who corrupted the earth by her adulteries. He has avenged on her the blood of his servants' is the roar of great multitudes (*Revelation 19:1–2*). He has fought our war.

Meditating on Isaiah's prophetic description of Messiah's final triumphant march in Isaiah 63:1-6, Thomas Kelly wrote his salute to our Lord Jesus as a man of war:

> Who is this that comes from Edom,
> All his raiment stained with blood;
> To the slave proclaiming freedom;
> Bringing and bestowing good;
> Glorious in the garb he wears,
> Glorious in the spoils he bears?
>
> 'Tis the Saviour, now victorious,
> Trav'ling onward in his might;
> 'Tis the Saviour, O how glorious
> To his people is the sight!
> Jesus now is strong to save,
> Mighty to redeem the slave.
>
> Why that blood his raiment staining?
> 'Tis the blood of many slain;
> Of his foes there's none remaining,
> None the conquest to maintain;
> Fall'n they are, no more to rise,
> All their glory prostrate lies.

Mighty Victor, reign for ever,
Wear the crown so dearly won;
Never shall thy people, Never
Cease to sing what thou hast done;
Thou hast fought thy people's foes;
Thou wilt heal thy people's woes.

David alludes to a very human difficulty experienced by those who have expended enormous energy in lion-hearted combat. He had felt a raging thirst that followed the employment of nearly super-human effort on a battlefield. Samson also understood this consequence of physical exertion in war. After killing a thousand Philistines with a jawbone of an ass for a weapon, 'he was very thirsty and cried out to the Lord, "You have given your servant this great victory. Must I now die of thirst and fall into the hands of the uncircumcised?"' (*Judges 15:18*). God heard and opened for Samson a spring to relieve his intense craving for water.

When Messiah crushes kings and rulers with heroic energy, 'He will drink from a brook beside the way; therefore he will lift up his head' (*vs. 7*). The Lord Jesus Christ will not stumble in the last day due to thirst. He will be refreshed (lifting up his head). Israel lost an opportunity to overtake her foes due to a foolish command from Saul that none should take refreshment (*1 Samuel 14:29,30*). When the Son of God goes to war on the last day no enemy will escape. He will be kept fresh for the fight with supplies of water beside the way.

There is a sharp contrast between the first and the second comings of Messiah. On his first visit to our planet 'God did not send his Son into the world to condemn the world, but to save the world through him' (*John 3:17*). He came with patience and pleading. He endured the vicious attacks of his enemies without complaint or expression of vengeance. He died crying, 'I thirst.' He invited all to eternal life, full and free. He preached that nations should repent to receive forgiveness for sins.

Even now, in the heavens, Jesus Christ patiently endures the evil belligerence of his enemies. They mock the Son of God, his Word, his servants. They persecute the Church. All this the Lord of glory suffers in order to gather to himself a people as numerous, as lovely, as fresh as the dew of dawn.

But the day of grace and longsuffering will end. The era of patience will close, as will the gate to life. The King at God's right hand will buckle on his sword. With a fire of wrath in his eye Messiah will enter the earth again. Everyone who obeyed not the gospel will be crushed beneath his heel. Every leader of wickedness he will personally confront and destroy. 'Who can stand when he appears?' Who will endure His indignation? None can survive the onslaught of the Man at God's right hand.

Men delude themselves with thoughts like, 'Where is this coming he promised? Ever since our fathers died, everything goes on as it has since the beginning of creation' (*2 Peter 3:4*). World War II was a bloody conflict. Yet the carnage purchased peace and freedom for multitudes. Christ will return to earth with his vesture dipped in blood. He will heap up the dead of the nations who oppose him, but in the fight he will purchase everlasting peace for all who trust him. He will take the earth away from the proud and give it to the meek. He will cast down the unbelieving and raise up men and women of faith. Christ will utterly extinguish the cause of the wicked.

At the hour when this world ends, the magnificent power of the Son of God will no longer be mysterious. Every eye will see Messiah robed in infinite might. Multitudes who worship him will pay homage to his invincible campaign. All who were not made willing subjects in the day of his spiritual power will fall beneath his feet to be broken. Each in his own way will magnify the King of kings and Lord of lords. To him alone be all glory both now and forever. To Jesus Christ will come the ultimate triumph and success. Every knee will bow under his might and every tongue ascribe victory to him.

HIS COMING AGAIN

'We wait for the blessed hope – the glorious appearing of our great God and Saviour, Jesus Christ.'   Titus 2:13

It is not clear that David wrote Psalm 45. Many believe he did not. But there is no conclusive evidence that the great psalmist of Israel was not the author. We cannot be certain whether this group of psalms (*42–49*) was composed by the Sons of Korah or assigned to them for use in public worship, since they were designated as Levitical performers of sacred music. When the entire group of psalms with similar headings is studied together, strong reasons arise to believe that David was the poet.

Figurative language based upon an ancient wedding forms the backdrop of this song. You must understand ancient Eastern wedding customs to appreciate the scene given to us by the prophet of long ago. Betrothal was the first social procedure leading to marriage in primitive times. It was usually arranged by the parents of both the bride and the groom, although, as we see in Bible stories of Isaac and Samson, parents often consulted the wishes of son and daughter. This was a much more serious step than is our modern custom of engagement. Terms of the marriage were agreed upon before witnesses. Bride and groom were committed to each other by oath. God's blessing was pronounced upon the union at this time. Thus we find that Joseph and Mary were called husband and wife even though their marriage was not physically consummated.

Something akin to divorce was needed to break the terms of betrothal.

An interval usually came between betrothal and the actual wedding. Time was commonly required to fulfil the terms of agreement at betrothal. For one thing, it was customary for the groom to pay a dowry to the father of the bride. You will recall that Jacob was expected to work seven years as payment for Rachel (*Genesis 29*).

When the actual wedding day came attendants of the bride would gather at her father's house. There she would adorn herself in her finest clothing. Attendants of the groom (usually both male and female) would gather at his home. He too would be dressed impressively. The wedding procession did not take place in a chapel but on the streets of the city. The groom and his companions would proceed to the bride's house. From there she and her entourage would be escorted back to the home of the groom. At the groom's house a joyful wedding feast was held. It was not unusual for these celebrations to last seven or fourteen days when the groom was of noble birth.

In Psalm 45 we are taken to a wedding procession. This is a royal ceremony, for the groom has a throne (*vs. 6*) and comes from palaces adorned with ivory (*vs. 8*). 'Daughters of kings are among your honoured women' (*vs. 9*) in this retinue. Verses 2–9 describe the stately spectacle of the king coming for his bride. Verses 10–15 are words of advice and encouragement to the waiting bride as the king comes into view. Verses 16 and 17 are a divine benediction pronounced on the marriage as the imperial couple enter the king's palace at the conclusion of their procession. There is great pomp and celebration!

Psalm 45: His Coming Again

When close attention is given to detail at this wedding procession to which we are admitted, it will become obvious that the King is none other than the Lord Jesus Christ. He came to this earth once to betroth a bride. He has paid a handsome sum to purchase her for himself. She, of course, is the Church of the Son of God. Having the hope of his returning to accompany her into his own ivory palaces, she is preparing herself. The day of Jesus' second coming will be the wedding day of the Lamb and his bride, the Church.

PROLOGUE

'My heart is stirred by a noble theme as I recite my verses for the king; my tongue is the pen of a skilful writer.'

Psalm 45:1

Our psalmist has been commissioned to be the official song-writer for the wedding day of the King of kings. He must compose music to be sung as the grandest wedding party of all ages makes its gala march before God and all his creation. Angels will crowd to this festal event. All eyes will turn to gaze on this spectacular occasion. Heaven and earth will bend its ear to listen to the poet's wedding hymn.

The song-writer is moved to the depths of his heart. He is devoted to his task. He is delighted with his chore. He is to write of nobility and love. His theme is to be the matchless affections of the most honourable Personage ever to grace this earth. He is eager to undertake his work. Words speedily trip off his tongue, for his whole heart is in this task. His song is from the heart, about the heart, and written to stir the hearts of his hearers.

[85]

1 : THE APPROACHING KING

Honoured as the psalmist is to write a poem to adorn the King's wedding, the artist must not put himself forward. It is not his task to display his talents but to bring all attention and praise to the king. His are to be 'verses for the king' (*vs. 1*). After his comment of verse 1 the poet is lost sight of behind the splendour of the bridegroom. Verses 2–9 take the vantage point of the bride. At the home of her youth she is watching as the procession comes into view. Our wedding song tells us how the King appears to the eye of his beloved.

Every Christian has 'turned to God from idols to serve the living and true God, and *to wait for his Son* from heaven, whom he raised from the dead – Jesus, who rescues us from the coming wrath' (*1 Thessalonians 1:9,10*). 'We *wait* for the blessed hope – the glorious appearing of our great God and Saviour, Jesus Christ' (*Titus 2:13*). 'Christ loved the church and gave himself up for her' (*Ephesians 5:25*). As he left this earth the first time, Jesus told his bride-to-be, 'I am going to prepare a place for you. And if I go and prepare a place for you, I will come back and take you to be with me that you also may be where I am' (*John 14:2,3*).

John the Apostle speaks at the start of his book of Revelation as if he were an attendant of the bride, standing with her in her father's house. Everyone there knows that the King is coming soon. But he is the first to catch a glimpse of the King's wedding party far off in the distance. 'Behold, he is coming with the clouds,' cries John (*Revelation 1:7*). His message is not that Jesus will one day come. Rather, he is on his way. The Church must rush to the window and look out.

Because the bride is expecting the King, there is great

excitement at the outcry. She has been waiting for him. She has been thinking of his promises and his affirmations of love. Now she must have a look at him. These early verses show the state of the bride's mind. The King is at the centre of all. Everything noticed through the lattice has to do with him. Mrs. A. R. Causin thus sets words of Samuel Rutherford's in metrical form:

> The bride eyes not her garment,
> But her dear bridegroom's face;
> I will not gaze at glory,
> But on my King of grace;
> Not at the crown he gifteth,
> But on his pierced hand:
> The Lamb is all the glory
> Of Emmanuel's land.

Joyful emotions should be roused in every Christian upon hearing again any Bible text which speaks of Messiah coming to take you to himself. Deep waves of emotions should wash upon the shore of your soul when you look at the bridegroom whose procession is approaching your house. Pleasant and joyful emotions should flow, especially as you contemplate who he is. Just so the song proceeds.

The King's Excellency

'You are the most excellent of men and your lips have been anointed with grace, since God has blessed you forever. All your robes are fragrant with myrrh and aloes and cassia; from palaces adorned with ivory the music of the strings makes you glad.'

Psalm 45:2,8

To the eye of one whose heart is filled with love, every detail of the King's person is most pleasing and most appealing. Scripture has taught us 'that when he appears . . . we shall see him as he is' (*1 John 3:2*). That immediate sight of Jesus may compel us to express the very words of our text. But even when members of his bride, by the Holy Spirit and through his Word, perceive with a spiritual insight what he is like who is coming again to receive us to himself, very similar expressions of appreciation for him overflow from our hearts.

When the Son of God is near, every spiritual sense within the bride is filled with delight. Her spiritual eye is taken with his lovely appearance. Verse 2 would better be translated, 'Fair, fair art thou above the sons of men'. Her spiritual ears are afforded deep pleasure by his speech. 'Your lips have been anointed with grace.' Her spiritual nostrils find his fragrance delectable. 'All your robes are fragrant.' Everything about Messiah is enjoyable to his Church. The bride's entire being relishes the exquisite sweetness that is found in him.

So handsome is the approaching King that a glance toward him while he is afar off compels her to cry out that his beauty has no equal in humanity. He is incomparable in splendour. Has that not been your assessment of every facet of Jesus' character? Each attribute is dazzling beyond all human standards. From whatever vantage point you look upon your Lord, he is radiant. If only you could keep him in view you would be filled with joy. As the woman cries in the Song of Solomon, 'How handsome you are!' (*1:16*); 'My lover is radiant and ruddy, outstanding among ten thousand' (*5:10*); 'He is altogether lovely' (*5:16*). 'No wonder the maidens love you! . . . How right they are to adore you!' (*1:3,4*).

Nothing, however, captivates the bride more than the King's manner of speech. Although God's Son is invested with infinite power and has a bearing of supreme manliness, he is not crude or brute-like. Jesus' conversation with his beloved is always gracious. His words charm her with gentleness and kindness. When first the Prince of glory found the Church, she was altogether covered with the blood of her sins. She was loathsome, with nothing in herself worthy to attract his interest or love. She had no excellence of character to commend herself to his holy dignity. Yet to her he spoke such words as, 'Your sins are forgiven.' 'Your faith has saved you; go in peace.' The relationship between Christ and his Church begins with gallant kindness from his mouth.

After his first sermon in the synagogue at Nazareth, 'All . . . were amazed at the gracious words that came from his lips' (*Luke 4:22*). 'The crowds were amazed at his teaching' (*Matthew 7:28*) throughout Jesus' public ministry. 'They were amazed. "Where did this man get this wisdom?" . . . they asked' (*Matthew 13:54*). 'Were not our hearts burning within us while he talked with us?' (*Luke 24:32*), they would say to each other.

When, in reading God's Word a Christian detects the speaking of his Lord, he is charmed by the grace upon Christ's lips. When, in hearing a Bible sermon, the preacher is forgotten and the soul cries, 'It is the voice of Jesus that I hear', how the soul is gratified with an awareness of his gentleness and grace. It is not an unusual experience for the bride to record: 'My heart began to pound for him . . . My heart had gone out to him when he spoke' (*Song of Solomon 5:4–6*). With what fondness the waiting bride cherishes the love notes of her coming King! His words are her meditation all the day.

Hearing these exclamations from the bride at her window should cause us to search our hearts. Do you have in your heart the elements of love to our Lord Jesus Christ? Have you seen in him a glory transcending any other known to man? Do you long for his appearing? Are his words precious to you because you have found them gracious? Is his presence attended by a rich, perfumed fragrance that draws out your heart to him? Is being near him the highest of all your pleasures? Can you say, 'Your love is more delightful than wine'? (*Song of Solomon 1:2*). Scripture pronounces 'grace to all who love our Lord Jesus Christ with an undying love' (*Ephesians 6:24*). But, 'If anyone does *not* love the Lord Jesus Christ, let him be accursed. O Lord, come!' (*1 Corinthians 16:22*).

The King's Victory

'Gird your sword upon your side, O mighty one; clothe yourself with splendour and majesty. In your majesty ride forth victoriously in behalf of truth, humility and righteousness; let your right hand display awesome deeds. Let your sharp arrows pierce the hearts of the king's enemies; let the nations fall beneath your feet.'

Psalm 45:3–5

After the bride notices the coming King's comeliness she observes his majestic strength. His bearing is that of military grandeur. Christ is mounted on a splendid steed. Girded upon his side and conspicuous is his sword. These are not the trappings of mere ceremony. Messiah is an august hero. He is 'the mighty one' fearful to behold. 'Who is this King of glory? The

Lord strong and mighty, the Lord mighty in battle . . . the Lord Almighty – he is the King of glory' (*Psalm 24:8, 10*). In distinguished battle garb he comes.

Just here a strange element enters this wedding procession. On his wedding day any warrior might well have his exploits celebrated in words like those of verses 4 and 5. If it were only a salute to his prowess as a champion in battle such descriptions would not be unusual. But our text is more serious than this. Messiah will slay enemies along the way during his wedding procession! He will not only look the part of a warrior in ceremonial uniform. He will ride victoriously, piercing the hearts of the King's enemies on his wedding march.

Revelation 19 joins together the wedding of the Lamb and the final conquest of the King of kings. The two events occur upon the same day. 2 Thessalonians 1:9 and 10 tell us that the wicked 'will be punished with everlasting destruction and shut out from the presence of the Lord and from the majesty of his power *on the day* he comes to be glorified in his holy people and to be marvelled at among all those who have believed'. Coming for his bride and destroying enemies are simultaneous.

Messiah's bride, living at some distance from his 'ivory palaces' is besieged by fierce and cruel enemies. The Church has fled into the desert from a vicious pursuing dragon (*Revelation 12:13, 14*). An enraged Satan is making war against all the poor woman's offspring – those who obey God's commands and hold to the testimony of Jesus (*Revelation 12:17*). The world, the flesh and the devil threaten her daily. In addition to this she is assaulted by death. The Church is dwelling in territory hostile to her and to the Lord to whom she is pledged. A wedding day is appointed. But Christ must ride into the jaws of his inveterate foes to take his bride to himself.

If the interval between betrothal and wedding day is to end, if the King of glory is to bring his bride into his chambers (*Song of Solomon 1:4*), then the final assault upon his enemies and hers must begin. Only as complete victory is his will the two lovers be united! Nations fall beneath Messiah's feet each step that he takes to embrace his bride. His dignity will reach its zenith just as her deliverance is complete. It is to rescue his precious bride that the Son of God goes forth to war.

Well does she trust confidently in him. He is mighty to save! The King at God's right hand is worthy of the Church's confidence. Majesty and power attend him as he rides. Messiah is victorious over every opponent. He is able to defend and provide for his lover who is waiting and watching for his conquering wedding procession.

Our wedding song tells us also that it is a noble cause for which the Bridegroom-Warrior enters combat. He is victorious 'in behalf of truth, humility and righteousness' (*vs. 4*). Messiah's adversaries and all those hostile to his bride represent forces of falsehood, pride and evil. Wicked is their resistance to the One who is King by divine right. Wicked is their denial and opposition to the truth and righteousness advocated by the Church. Vile is the oppression of the humble by the proud. The waiting and watching Church confidently expects a conquering King who will pierce the hearts of evil men so that she may be in fact as described in verse 9, 'at your right hand is the royal bride in gold of Ophir'. Soon she will be seated at the right hand of her victorious Lord!

[92]

The King's Destiny

'Your throne, O God, will last for ever and ever; a
sceptre of justice will be the sceptre of your kingdom.
You love righteousness and hate wickedness; therefore
God, your God, has set you above your companions by
anointing you with the oil of joy. All your robes are
fragrant with myrrh and aloes and cassia; from palaces
adorned with ivory the music of the strings makes you
glad. Daughters of kings are among your honoured
women; at your right hand is the royal bride in gold of
Ophir.'

Psalm 45:6–9

Watching and waiting for her Lord, the bride sees her
coming King afar off. There are glimmers of his glory
and of his triumph. Her heart cries, 'Tell him I am faint
with love' (*Song of Solomon 5:8*). Then the waiting
Church contemplates the King's home, his own palace,
his seat of power. When his wedding-war-procession
is ended, he will escort his bride to his abode. There she
will share the glories and honours which are his.

As we Christians await the loving approach of our
Lord our home is in a kingdom of impermanence and
decay. All is temporary, changing and dying. There is a
woeful disintegration to the material world constantly
observable in our very bodies. Rulers rise to power
only to fall once more. Societies gain strength only to
crumble. Even churches constantly show signs of
decline and collapse. Nothing is enduring. Our
sojourn here is fleeting.

When Messiah's procession arrives at the door of
our house, earth, he will usher his bride into his
everlasting kingdom. God has blessed his Son forever
(*vs. 2b*). 'Your throne, O God, will last for ever and

ever' (*vs. 6*). Here is one of the clearest Bible texts in which Messiah is called 'God' (*Elohim*) in the form of direct address. The bridegroom has a beauty 'above that of men' (*vs. 2*) because he is infinitely more noble in being. He is God, God incarnate. The eternal Son of God must have an everlasting throne! His kingdom will in no way disappear, spoil, or fade. There will be no rotting or dilapidation attached to him, his subjects, his society, his government. 'Of the increase of his government and peace there will be no end. He will reign on David's throne and over his kingdom, establishing and upholding it with justice and righteousness from that time on and forever' (*Isaiah 9:7*). The queen will dwell with him in his *everlasting* domain. She too will have everlasting life.

While the Church in readiness eagerly watches for the returning Saviour, she must endure an environment of injustice. Many believers and their friends are mistreated and oppressed. Too often criminals and rulers conspire to overwhelm the meek. Our homeland in this present world is impatient with conscientious righteousness. Rather it embraces wickedness and rewards ungodly behaviour. Due to the topsy-turvy world system, the king's bride is frequently brought to deep sorrow. She suffers herself and weeps for others who are wronged.

Victorious Messiah will crush the evil nations when he comes for his bride. Then she will be whisked under the shadow of her bridegroom's sceptre. 'A sceptre of justice will be the sceptre of your kingdom' (*vs. 6*). In his empire not one will be mistreated. Each citizen will receive his due with even-handed fairness. 'You love righteousness and hate wickedness; therefore God, your God, has set you above your companions' (*vs. 7*).

The balance will be turned in his dynasty. Truth and righteousness will prevail. All wickedness will be expunged. 'Nothing impure will ever enter his nation' (*Revelation 21:27*). His bride will enjoy with him this pure and utterly equitable state forever.

Because of the curse upon her homeland, because of ruin, because of injustice and sin the bride waits for her Lord in ominous surroundings. She must confront much that is ugly. It is impossible to avoid all that is false, impure, ignoble and wrong. Sorrow fills her heart at thoughts of the shameful and despicable events of her realm. Suffering and poverty touch her life. But as she views the approach of her betrothed King she anticipates the radical change which is about to take place.

The King's palace is a place of richness and beauty. It is 'adorned with ivory' (*vs. 8*). His queen is richly robed in gold (*vs. 9*). His own robes are all fragrant with pleasant spices (*vs. 8*). Joyful music of stringed instruments fills the atmosphere (*vs. 8*). The King, having been anointed with joy (*vs. 7*), shares his uninterrupted happiness with those who are with him. Only noble society is to be found there. 'Daughters of kings are among your honoured women' (*vs. 9*) at court. Nothing of poverty, sorrow or ugliness will have a part in his throne-room. Best of all she will be 'at your right hand' (*vs. 9*) forevermore. She will never again be forced to part from him whom her heart loves (*Song of Solomon 3:1*). She will be forever with the Lord (*1 Thessalonians 4:17*). It will be a blissfully happy condition.

Paul speaks about those 'who have longed for his [Jesus'] appearing' (*2 Timothy 4:8*). They are strangers and pilgrims on the earth. They are looking for a city with foundations, whose builder and maker is God. They are keenly aware that this world is not their home and never will yield them joy and satisfaction. They are expecting the King to come back for them and to take them to his palace to be with him in fellowship evermore. They will never be content with anything else. They will not be bribed to be at peace in the present world, not by pleasures, honours, or material possessions. Theirs is 'an inheritance incorruptible, undefiled and that does not fade away, reserved in heaven' (*1 Peter 1:4*). It is the King's wedding present to his bride, the Church.

Some saints have been waiting long for their Master's return, for the wedding procession. But love 'burns like blazing fire, like a mighty flame. Many waters cannot quench love; rivers cannot wash it away. If one were to give all the wealth of his house for love, it would be utterly scorned' (*Song of Solomon 8:6,7*). The Son of God loved me and gave himself for me (*Galatians 2:20*). Now 'we love because he first loved us' (*1 John 4:19*). 'My lover is mine and I am his' (*Song of Solomon 2:16*). Behold, he is coming! And we are waiting.

> When he comes, our glorious King,
> All his ransomed home to bring,
> Then anew this song we'll sing,
> Hallelujah! What a Saviour!

2: THE AWAITING BRIDE

Watching as the King's wedding procession comes into view, the bride's heart is warmed by his beauty and grace. She admires anew her beloved's triumphant strength. She daydreams pleasantly of her Lord's kingdom and palace. There is sweetness and comfort in all these thoughts about Messiah. Yet those who stand by her, those who have been assisting her preparations for the wedding day, notice in the bride's countenance a hint of nervousness and misgiving.

Although the Church adores the King, although she has full confidence in his goodness and power, although she has no doubt of the supreme happiness of dwelling in his presence, there are self-doubts. Every member of the Church has been given the spiritual gifts of meekness and humility. These qualities are of great worth in the sight of the bridegroom, but they do create uncertainty within herself. There is hesitation. Is she indeed ready to forsake her present home to go with the King? Self-distrust comes to mind even at this last moment. A still more serious difficulty fills her thoughts. Will the King be pleased with me? How can so majestic a dignitary want me for his wife?

Bridal Assurance

'Listen, O daughter, consider and give your ear: Forget your people and your father's house. The king is enthralled by your beauty; honour him, for he is your lord. The Daughter of Tyre will come with a gift, men of wealth will seek your favour.'

Psalm 45:10–12

Wise attendants to the bride are aware of a young woman's doubts on her wedding day. They have been watching for the first disturbed look, the first suggestion of sadness. She must not be left alone to muse introspectively. Her helpers call her away from the window and engage her in conversation. More is

needed than assistance in dressing for her King.
Judicious counsellors must wait upon her to encourage
and reassure the King's beloved.

There are times when false doctrine and hypocrisy
abound even within Christ's Church. Then very
searching and convicting preaching is called for. When
those who are pledged to Christ by baptism grow
weary of waiting and forget to watch, an alarm must be
sounded. When preparations for the Lamb's wedding
day have fallen into neglect, the bride must be jolted
with warnings.

However, severe tones must not mark all the words
of those who assist the bride in her preparations for
Christ. When meekness and humility do mark her
spirit, her ministers must be sensitive to her deep need
for confidence. How we must learn to speak to one
another in the mood of these verses. Ministers of the
gospel must perceive that there are many true-hearted
saints who love the Lord Jesus sincerely and who
struggle with very deep self-doubts. These do not need
more thunder but rather gentle, confidence-building
words.

Secret meditations of the bride are interrupted by the
words, 'Listen, O daughter . . .'. The speaker is older
than she and affectionately looks upon her as a
daughter. Uncertainty often comes with youth. Un-
realistic idealism makes impossible demands upon
one in youth and leaves the spirit uneasy. A lack of
experiencing the goodness, forbearance and faith-
fulness of the Lord brings to the young believer
unnecessary imaginations of personal failure and rejection by the Lord. An older counsellor can be so
reassuring. The bride will be surrounded with beautiful young maidens on her wedding day, but the aged

can do some things for her which her young friends cannot.

Perhaps the speaker is the very one who travailed in bringing the bride to the birth (*Galatians 4:19*). With special interest and most tender love would this adviser speak. Deeply involved in betrothal arrangements, the voice of sage advice has pledged her to Christ. Are not gospel ministers those who agonize until hearers are born again? In evangelism and counselling do they not labour to betroth their people to Christ. Who then can better reassure the waiting bride as God's Son approaches?

'Consider and give ear' is urged upon this daughter in the faith. How difficult to secure the heartfelt attention of the doubting Christian. Self-recriminations may so captivate the thoughts of the humble that outside counsel can scarcely reach the heart. 'Listen!' 'Consider!' 'Give ear!' Pay attention. Do not allow your inner doubts to drown out my last words of advice to you. It is only a short time until the King will be here. Now consider what I say. We must rouse those whose minds have drawn within themselves in gloomy distrust of self.

'Forget your people and your father's house.' Christ's church is placed in much the same position as was Rebekah, the daughter of Bethuel (*Genesis 24*). You will remember that a servant of Abraham came from a far country to betroth her to Isaac. To marry the heir of a wealthy estate and a gracious covenant, she was called upon to leave her parents, family, friends and known world, to travel to a distant place. When the servants of God come to make the proposition that we marry God's Son, it involves forsaking all to go with the King to his inheritance.

Wise and experienced counsel in the ear of the maiden is to forget all and choose Christ. Christian, you have made the correct choice! It is the best possible decision to sell all else and secure Christ. Nothing can be compared to having him. It is shrewd judgment which led you to turn your back on parents, children, friends, earthly pleasures, meagre temporal riches and all to be Christ's bride.

If the one addressing the bride is a married woman, the advice is all the more weighty. She too once left all to belong to her husband. She is telling the bride on her wedding day, 'It is the right choice.' Your marriage will bring you such glorious joys that the cost of leaving your present world cannot compare with what you will gain.

When first the Prince of glory came to seek her hand, the Church concluded that she loved God's Son and would be pledged to him. She knew then that she must 'forsake all that she has' (*Luke 14:33*) to go with him. Still the delay of the wedding procession brings many moments of reconsidering. It is painful to leave behind mother and father, son and daughter. We are attached to the beauties and friendships of this world. 'Forget' them all! The King will more than make up for all. Some day you will look back upon the parting with temporal things and think your hesitation silly and ill-founded. When you sit in the ivory palace, arrayed in the gold of Ophir, at the right hand of the eternal King, you will wonder what you saw in those former things. You will never regret it!

Taking up a cross will seem to be no burden but rather a sail to carry you to your desired haven. Denying yourself of earthly things will be a paltry price to pay for heavenly delights. A loss of earthly friends will soon be forgotten in the company of kings' daughters and in the embraces of your Lord. Think no more of what you leave behind. You have chosen the better lot. Carry through with your discerning choice. Put all the past behind you and fill your mind with the glories that await. The King must be your one and only love henceforth. He must have all your heart and devotion.

What tender insight into the Christian's unspoken fears marks the next words of reassurance! 'The King is enthralled by your beauty.' The meek and humble Church can think of ten thousand reasons why she should be charmed by Christ. As she recounts his loveliness and grace she is ever more spellbound with him. But the Church can think of no reason why the King should be enamoured with her. Although our hearts would burst if we did not profess our love to the Anointed of the Lord, we find it difficult to think that he would be attracted to us.

After all, those who are now saints were born in trespasses and sins. Guilty of original sin, vile with pollution of all our being, and helpless to do anything good in God's sight, we were the slaves of sin. Our past was spotted with rebellion against the authority of Messiah and his Father. Our entire complexion was blemished from a hatred that coursed through our veins. When first the Holy Spirit opened our eyes by the Word, we looked into a mirror and saw ourselves ugly and repulsive. Never did we imagine that the King would fall in love with us. We only thought that his iron sceptre would fall upon us and rid him of our abhorrent presence.

Having sought pardoning mercy by bowing before the throne of Christ under the terrors of the law's curses, it has taken many tender words of Scripture to make us even begin to think that we are the objects of his affections. We have for the Saviour who granted us life a raging fire of love that many oceans of water could not quench. But it is still astounding to us to hear the suggestion that there is in him a spark of love to us. He has not dealt with us according to our sins but with enormous gentleness and tender mercy. There is no harshness or bitterness in God's Son. Overwhelming grace flows from his lips. But it is another thing to become convinced that he is in love with me!

Jesus' bride collects many love notes from her beloved. She keeps in her box of jewels little scraps on which are written, 'I have loved you with an everlasting love; I have drawn you with lovingkindness' (*Jeremiah 31:3*). These are signed, 'The Lord'. Other bits of paper read, 'Greater love has no one than this, that he lay down his life for his friends. You are my friends' (*John 15:13,14*), and, 'the Son of God, who loved me and gave himself for me' (*Galatians 2:20*), and, 'Father, I want those you have given me to be with me where I am' (*John 17:24*), and, 'having loved his own who were in the world, he loved them to the end' (*John 13:1*). These give her hope.

It would make the bride blush if you were to read the words from her Lord which she keeps next to her heart. They run something like this, 'How beautiful you are, my darling! Oh, how beautiful!' (*Song of Solomon 1:15*). 'Your voice is sweet, and your face is lovely' (*2:14*). 'Like a lily among thorns is my darling among the maidens' (*2:2*). 'How delightful is your love . . . How much more pleasing is your love than wine' (*4:10*). 'You have stolen my heart' (*4:9*). 'The king is held captive' (*7:5*).

In better moments the saints believe the love Christ has for his Church. At other times, with smiles, the bride asks, 'How can he be enthralled with me?' At still others, especially after having fallen into the mire and having seen her spots in the mirror, she has flashbacks to the hours of horror under the Holy Spirit's convicting work. Then for all her Lord's love-letters she is unsure that they were meant for her. Perhaps she has been confused with another. What could he possibly see in her? Perhaps the King will arrive on the wedding day only to disapprove of her and cast her aside. Perhaps the union will never be consummated.

Hence friends close to the bride must constantly remind her that the Mighty King is enchanted by her beauty. Did he not die for her? Does he not ever live to intercede for her? Did he not swear to return for her? Is love for her not the moving force of Messiah's victory march? The Church is the most beautiful of women (*Song of Solomon 1:8, 5:9, 6:1*). Meek and humble saints require constant reassurance until confidence is strong once more, confidence that the King's desire is for the Church. 'The King is enthralled by your beauty.'

Advisers to the church add, 'Honour him, for he is your Lord.' The word translated 'honour' is literally 'bow down' to him. It is the most pertinent reminder that could be given to a bride on her wedding day. This is not the 'love' story of a steamy sex novel, in which nothing but illicit physical passion exists between man and woman. This is true love, pure and noble love. The King exercises his power for truth and righteousness (*vs. 4*). His marriage will follow the commands of God's truth. His relationship with his bride will display moral integrity.

There are double reasons for the Church to bow to Christ. Jesus Christ, risen from the dead, has been made Lord of the earth and its nations. All the ends of the world must revere him, for his is uncontestable, God-given authority. As part of humanity, Messiah's domain, the bride must bow to her Lord. But she is also pledged to be his wife. God's Son is Lord as ruler of her world, but he is also Lord as her husband. Everywhere, in Old Testament and New, God has taught that wives must reverence their husbands and submit to them (*Ephesians 5:22–33; Colossians 3:18; 1 Peter 3:1–6; Genesis 3:16*).

If a marriage union is to endure, the husband must express his love to his wife by tenderly cherishing her as part of his own body, by considerateness, by sharing all the goodness of God in his life with her. She in turn must express love by holding her husband in high esteem and by submitting to him in all things. Thus the Church must bow down to Christ both because he is her Lord and Sovereign and because he is her Lord and Husband. Since the bride loves her Lord, it is a pleasant thing to serve his interests. She desires to bring Christ honour, to fulfil his will, to worship his name.

Other fluttering attendants, excited with the nearness of the King's procession, tell the bride, 'The Daughter of Tyre will come with a gift, men of wealth will seek your favour.' What dignity and influence will be hers in a very short time! Those who esteem the King will seek her out. Gifts will be brought to the King's wife from all over the earth. She will be asked by the nations to appeal to her husband on their behalf.

Already the prayers of the saints move their Lord. Even now the Church pleads the cause of the Gentiles and seeks Christ's favour for them. Because of her union with Christ, great dignitaries come to the Church. What renown is about to be hers when she dwells in the palace of the King and sits with him upon the throne! The bride is about to take the loftiest position a mere creature can assume.

Bridal Appearance

'*All glorious is the princess within her chamber; her gown is interwoven with gold. In embroidered garments she is led to the king; her virgin companions follow her and are brought to you.*'

Psalm 45:13–15

God's Son has come from his distant palace. His procession made a splendid sight. As he was yet far off the bride watched with leaping heart. Her mighty Lord has delivered her from her oppressors as he came. The last enemies he destroyed were death and hell. Attendants called her away from the window to soothe her troubled spirit. But now the last words of counsel have been spoken. Her bridegroom is at the door.

'All glorious is the princess within', says the Scripture. Translators feel compelled to add 'within her chamber' (*N.I.V.*) or 'within the palace' (*N.K.J.*). Immediately the text adds 'her gown is interwoven with gold', perhaps suggesting that she is meticulously attired within and without. She has more than external splendour. There is inward beauty.

No wonder the King is held captive by the bride! It now becomes evident why she is pleasing and delightful to him, why with one glance of her eyes she steals his heart (*Song of Solomon 4:9*). She has purified herself and made herself ready for the King.

Messiah personally provided the garments for his bride. 'Christ loved the church and gave himself up for her to make her holy, cleansing her by the washing with water through the word, and to present her to himself as a radiant church, without stain or wrinkle or any other blemish, but holy and blameless' (*Ephesians 5:25–27*). He sent his Holy Spirit to give her 'the washing of rebirth and renewal by the Holy Spirit' (*Titus 3:5*). By the Spirit's work of regeneration a decisive process of purification was begun. Through the blood of the Son of God, his Church was given radical sanctification at the new birth.

However, sanctification is not completed all at once. When the bride is made a new creation she comes to hope that she will see the Lord at his return. 'We know that when he [Jesus] appears we shall be like him, for we shall see him as he is. Everyone who has this hope in him purifies himself, just as he is pure' (*1 John 3:2,3*). All who truly hope to see Jesus return for them are actively purifying themselves. Using the means of grace there is constant progress: 'washing with water through the word'. At conversion the Christian's purity is like the first gleam of day. There is enormous contrast between light at dawn and dark night. But the sun rises more and more until it arrives at the noon-day zenith of brilliance. 'The path of the righteous is like the first gleam of dawn, shining ever brighter till the full light of day' (*Proverbs 4:18*).

That part of God's Word which most beautifies the bride in her progressive sanctification is the revelation of Christ himself. 'We are being transformed into his likeness with ever increasing glory' (*2 Corinthians 3:18*) by gazing upon his glory. However, the progressive nature of sanctification will end abruptly when the

bride opens her door to the King and looks him full in
the face. Instantaneously the last spot will disappear
and the last wrinkle will be gone. In seeing him as he is
we shall be fully like him in the beauty of holiness
(*1 John 3:2*).

From its inception this sanctifying process is of the
Lord Jesus. The King himself shed his blood to purify
us, sent his Spirit to purify us, gave the means of grace to
purify us. At the first moment of our cleansing, the work
was lovely to the eyes of Christ. In every degree of
progress our sanctification is beautiful to him. And
when glorified with flawless righteousness the King will
be captivated by his bride's beauty.

Her preparations have not been in mere outward
appearances. Christ's bride keeps her heart with all
diligence, knowing that from it are the issues of life
(*Proverbs 4:23*). She has first given her heart to the Lord,
then externals have followed. Unlike the Pharisees
whose purification has to do with separation from
external objects, and washing only the outside of the
cup, the Church is all glorious within. Messiah's bride
gives close attention to her inner attire, for the
bridegroom will be ravished with that.

It is no wonder then, that with such inward, spiritual
care she is so striking without. Her gown is interwoven
with pure gold. It is radiant beauty of righteousness
within and without. 'In embroidered garments she is led
to the king'. When he looks at her the King thinks, 'My
darling, my dove, my flawless one' (*Song of Solomon
5:2*). His heart thinks of the bride, 'All beautiful you are,
my darling; there is no flaw in you' (*4:7*). He is utterly
delighted with the Church he has presented to himself!

Christ is depicted as having arrived at the house of his
bride, the Church. She is led out to the King! Her virgin

companions follow behind her in splendid procession. Her mighty Lord has crushed all his and her enemies in his approach to take her to himself. The exquisite moment of the groom and the bride meeting is one of breathless joy.

Always the Church has viewed the glory of her King from afar. Most have believed on him, never having seen with their eyes, never having been privileged to be in his immediate presence. But the moment will come when the Church will gaze full in his wonderful face. Her Lord will be there. Most Christians have been like Rebekah. A messenger representing the Lord who dwells afar off has come to betroth her to him. We have received the pledges of love and fidelity sight unseen. Imagine what it will be to see him of whom you have heard so much, for whom you have forsaken your father's house, your known world, your all! You will look upon him for whose coming your life has been a preparation.

She is led out to the King. This is the moment of marriage. He is to take her to himself for the procession back to the palace. Publicly, before all the astounded world of angels and nations the Christ gallantly receives the bride. Now it is one thing for a sinner to receive Jesus as his Lord. It is infinitely more marvellous to behold the Lord receive the transformed sinner as his beloved bride. The Church has identified herself with the Lord of glory before a world that despises him. The King will openly espouse her as his wife forever – as God the Father looks on, as pure and fallen angels observe, as impenitent but subdued sinners are spectators. Jesus Christ will own his Church, will take her to himself. At that instant the union is publicly complete.

No wonder the New Testament repeatedly returns to this description of the Christian: 'We wait for the

blessed hope – the glorious appearing of our great God
and Saviour, Jesus Christ . . . ' (*Titus 2:13*). We have
been called to serve the living and true God, and 'to
wait for his Son from heaven' (*1 Thessalonians
1:9–10*). Is the expectation of his coming the motive of
your purifying yourself? Are you looking for his
arrival with eager anticipation?

In her spiritual longings the bride often grows
impatient. 'Let us hurry! Let the king bring me into his
chambers' (*Song of Solomon 1:4*). The age of revelation
closes with Christ calling out to the Church, 'Yes, I am
coming soon.' The bride heartily responds, 'Amen.
Come, Lord Jesus' (*Revelation 22:20*). The echo of
Jesus' last words to us rings in our hearts. Each
Christian ever cries, 'Come quickly, Lord Jesus.'

3: THE APPROVAL OF THE UNION

*'They are led in with joy and gladness; they enter the
palace of the king. Your sons will take the place of your
fathers; you will make them princes throughout the
land. I will perpetuate your memory through all
generations; therefore the nations will praise you
forever and ever.'*

Psalm 45:15–17

With one brush stroke of poetry the psalmist hurries
our imagination through the return procession and
into the wedding feast of the Lamb. After describing
the bride being led to the king outside her house, his
next words are of the bride and groom being led into
his palace. Is it too much to imagine the return
procession to the palace of Messiah?

Back through the regions of conquered enemies they
ride in regal dignity. Attended with legions of angels

[109]

the Lord and his Church are hailed with joy and celebration. Their greatness together is acclaimed all along the way. Defeated foes watch in helpless ruin. Observing is the sceptic who once sneered that there was no reality to the Church's trust in this unseen King. All who laughed at the faith of the bride will watch her pass by at the side of her Lord, taken by him to be his holy bride. All who preferred a fallen world system with its pleasures and riches will sit amidst the ruins and ashes of that temporary order now demolished. They will lift their shameful heads to see the Church in a gown interwoven with gold, all radiant in the presence of her loving Lord, about to enter his kingdom and hers. No doubt will remain in any soul of the wisdom of waiting for Messiah and the foolishness of having scorned his offers of mercy. But the Church will pass them by. At that moment those who are accursed will be accursed still. They will have forever to envy the Church and regret their tragic rejection of her society on earth.

At the palace of the King all is joy and gladness! The King himself will say to the bride, 'Come, you who are blessed by my Father, take your inheritance, the kingdom prepared for you since the creation of the world' (*Matthew 25:34*), and, 'Come and share your master's happiness' (*Matthew 25:21*). The palace will be fully adorned. Messiah himself has seen to the preparations (*John 14:2*). The music of strings is playing to make the bride glad (*Psalm 45:8*). All who are assembled are in a festive mood.

There will be so many great streams feeding into the ocean of pleasure which the bride will feel at that moment. She will be satisfied with her own beauty at that moment, for she will have received it all of grace. It will be an enormous pleasure to be fully prepared in righteousness for the Messiah. She will be 'beautifully dressed for her husband' (*Revelation 21:2*). She will be shining 'with the glory of God' and have a 'brilliance . . . like that of a very precious jewel' (*Revelation 21:11*). 'All glorious within . . . a gown interwoven with gold' (*Psalm 45:13*). The King will be enthralled with her beauty. She will feel deep joy in it, too.

Another stream of gladness for the bride will be awareness that she is admitted to his dwelling place after so long a separation from the King. What transports of joy to be with him, never again to be parted. She will be 'forever with the Lord' to share his life and to gaze and gaze upon him! 'Now the dwelling of God is with men . . . God himself will be with them' (*Revelation 21:3*). 'They will see his face' (*Revelation 22:4*), being constantly in his company. He will not go away again, ever. How blessed will be the pure in heart, for they will see God (*Matthew 5:8*). It shall be joy unspeakable.

All godly husbands realize that their wives are 'heirs with you of the gracious gift of life' (*1 Peter 3:7*). The Lord from heaven will share all of his life and inheritance with the bride. It will no longer be only the palace of the King but *their* palace. The Church will 'reign with him for ever and ever' (*Revelation 22:5*). As Christ sits at the right hand of God the Father Almighty, believers in Jesus will sit at his right hand. There they will share his dignity, privileges and infinite riches forever. Surely there will be a smile on the lips of the bride when she who suffered with Christ begins to reign with him (*2 Timothy 2:12*).

In this palace of righteousness, peace, and joy in the Holy Spirit the bride's joy and gladness will be full. She will begin an eternity of intimate communion with God the Son. From a fallen world to the palace of the King, the ultimate rags to riches account – and it is true! From the dung-heap of sin to the palace of the King, by his grace.

In every age the most joyful social occasion is a wedding feast. Hence Scripture has chosen the marriage celebration to depict the full delight of God's people when they enter the presence of their Lord and Saviour. At the marriage supper we reach the highest peaks of joy and hope and pleasant expectations.

Usually family members and friends assemble for the festivities. They too share the joy of their loved ones. All round the world it is customary to offer toasts, express good wishes and pronounce benedictions upon the bride and groom. The feast which is held at the palace of the King is no different. A blessing is pronounced upon the King. It involves his bride, for the two have become one to share all good things in life.

A place of honour is given to the greatest dignitaries at the feast. They are given the privilege of being the first to offer congratulations to the wedded couple. In the palace of the King, a tribute rings out at the start of the feast. Its words are recorded in the last two verses of our psalm. No doubt, it is the blessing of the Almighty upon Messiah who has taken his bride! A divine benediction.

Some poor brides enter upon their marriages under the stress of reluctant approval, or even disapproval, by the groom's family. Not so with the Church. She was personally chosen by God the Father to be the holy bride of his Son. His electing love gave her to the Son. This benediction comes from One who loved both the King and his bride with eternal love, love which flowed before the foundation of the world. The Most High is unreservedly pleased with this union. He planned it of old and is deeply gratified that it has come to pass.

However, the pronouns in Jehovah's blessing are masculine. He is speaking most directly to Messiah. This union will issue in numerous seed or 'sons'. Poetry may speak of one and the same Christians as a 'bride' at one moment, and as 'sons' the next. We who believe in Christ are both the Church and the sons of the Church. We are the body of Christ and the children of Christ.

What the Father speaks to Messiah is in one sense retrospective. It is not altogether future to the marriage feast of the Lamb. There is a comparison between Old Testament progenitors of Messiah and New Testament offspring of Messiah. The sons of the Church are to be more numerous and more illustrious than the ancestors of Jesus. The Mosaic covenant was glorious but the Messianic covenant is surpassing in glory. The Church, unlike the Jewish state, stretches over the whole earth to its utmost parts. Sons of the gospel 'take the place' of the fathers of Messiah's humanity. They are princes by comparison through-out all nations.

This interpretation is reinforced by verse 17 where we are told that 'the nations will praise you forever and ever'. Eternal anthems of worship are offered to the King by men of every nation, family, tribe and language! A multitude that no man can number are the sons of Messiah! Every one of them is a prince. If Abraham, Isaac, Jacob, David, Solomon, all were glorious, their greatness has been supplanted by the offspring of Christ and the Church. The least in the kingdom of God is greater than the most outstanding of the fathers.

Do you feel insignificant, Christian? Do you feel unattractive to the eye of Christ? Do you feel discouraged in a world of sin, persecution, obscurity and suffering? Your Lord is drawing near! At his coming and in his palace you will view reality so differently. Make this promise-studded psalm your meditation. Keep it near to your heart. It will be your consolation and delight.

A Biblical description of Messiah makes him terrifying to all who reject him because they love wickedness rather than light. Yet all who acknowledge themselves sinners and come to him for mercy will discover him tender, compassionate, and loving beyond description. How is it that some find him a rock upon which they are built to receive eternal life while others are offended at him and stumble to their destruction? How varied the pictures of the King, a mighty warrior dashing his enemies to pieces and a loving groom taking his bride.

'"See, I lay a stone in Zion, a chosen and precious cornerstone, and the one who trusts in him will never be put to shame." Now to you who believe, this stone is precious. But to those who do not believe, "The stone the builders rejected has become the capstone," and, "a stone that causes men to stumble and a rock that makes them fall." They stumble because they disobey the message – which is also what they were destined for. But you are a chosen people, a royal priesthood, a holy nation, a people belonging to God, that you may declare the praises of him who called you out of darkness into his wonderful light' (*1 Peter 2:6–9*). May the Messianic psalms enable you to worship your Lord with ever-deepening warmth and admiration, until he comes.

SOME OTHER
BANNER OF TRUTH
TITLES

SIGNS OF THE APOSTLES
Walter Chantry

How should the Christian assess contemporary claims about spiritual gifts? Walter Chantry believes that God is still working in the world today. But it is his conviction that miraculous powers are no longer placed in the hands of individual men and women.

Tracing the occurrence of miracles in the Old and New Testaments, he concludes that their function was primarily to attest the commission of the spokesman of God. This is why, he maintains, every recorded instance of the reception of miraculous power in the New Testament Church occurred through the ministry of an Apostle. Now that the canon of Scripture is complete, Walter Chantry believes that the pursuit of all the spiritual gifts of the apostolic age can only proceed upon the basis of a failure to recognize the sufficiency and finality of the Bible.

Walter Chantry was born in 1938 at Norristown, Pennsylvania, raised in the Presbyterian Church; graduated B.A. in History from Dickinson College, Carlisle in 1960, and B.D. from Westminster Theological Seminary in 1963, from which time he has been pastor of Grace Baptist Church, Carlisle.

ISBN 0 85151 175 9
160pp., paperback

GOD'S RIGHTEOUS KINGDOM
The Law's Connection with the Gospel
Walter Chantry

The Gospel is always open to two abuses – legalism, on the one hand, which destroys the saving grace of God, and antinomianism on the other, which sets grace against the responsibility to obedience in the Christian.

In the space of twelve chapters, Walter Chantry expounds the relationship of the Law to the Gospel in a way which touches contemporary controversy; but he does so through painstaking exposition of the Scriptures, so that his message has abiding relevance. In particular he deals with the kind of question which troubles many ordinary Christians – Were there two ways of salvation in the Old and New Testaments? Do the Old Testament laws all apply in the same way today, or do they apply to us at all? What was Jesus' attitude to the Law? How does the Sabbath day fit in?

Short chapters, clearly argued, written in a popular style and with practical applications always in mind, this is a book with an important message for contemporary Christians.

ISBN 0 85151 310 7
154pp., paperback

TODAY'S GOSPEL
Authentic or Synthetic?
Walter Chantry

In this arousing work Walter Chantry expounds from Christ's dealing with the Rich Young Ruler the essential elements in Gospel preaching. A close examination of the Scripture evidence leads to this conclusion:

'Differences between much of today's preaching and that of Jesus are not petty; they are enormous. The chief errors are not in emphasis or approach but in the heart of the Gospel message. Were there a deficiency in one of the areas mentioned in these pages, it would be serious. But to ignore all – the attributes of God, the holy law of God, repentance, a call to bow to the enthroned Christ – and to pervert the doctrine of assurance, is the most vital mistake.

'Incredulity may grip you. Can so many evangelicals be so wrong? . . . All are not in error, but great hosts are. All have not perverted the gospel to the same degree, but many are terribly far from the truth. All those who "make decisions" are not deceived, but great numbers are. Above all, few *care* to recover the Gospel message . . .'.

This powerfully-written book has a message which goes to the heart of the contemporary problem in a way that conferences and commissions on evangelism have failed to do. Its expository approach is particularly valuable.

ISBN o 85151 027 2
96pp., paperback

THE SHADOW OF THE CROSS
Studies in Self-Denial
Walter Chantry

The message of the Cross is the heart of the Christian gospel. The records of the life of Jesus devote more attention to it than any other part of his ministry. The rest of the New Testament constantly underlines its centrality for Christian faith.

But Jesus and the apostles spoke of 'the cross' as a principle of Christian experience as well as the chief symbol of God's love. Belonging to Jesus Christ (he said) meant taking up the cross personally and living for him rather than for ourselves.

In *The Shadow of the Cross*, Walter J. Chantry restores this often neglected teaching to its central place. Writing with the stirring and probing sharp-edged style which is the hall mark of all his books, it expounds in brief compass the practical necessity of bearing the cross and the joy of living under its shadow. He then applies this to such areas as marriage, Christian liberty, the work of the ministry and prayer.

ISBN 0 85151 331 X
80pp., paperback

A HEART FOR GOD
Sinclair B. Ferguson

A Heart for God is written out of the conviction that the world's greatest need – and the contemporary church's greatest lack – is the knowledge of God. In a popular, readable style it draws us to an awareness of the character of God and the nature of his relationship to his people.

In these pages, Sinclair B. Ferguson guides us, step-by-step, to see the greatness of God in his majesty and creating power; to sense the tenderness of his care and the marvel of his love. *A Heart for God* is 'Practical, pastoral and profound' (J. I. Packer). It unfolds the grace of God with a simple clarity which should lead each reader to pray (with John Calvin, the reformer): 'I offer my heart to you, Lord, eagerly and earnestly.'

Dr Sinclair B. Ferguson is Professor of Systematic Theology at Westminster Theological Seminary, Philadelphia, U.S.A., and is the author of a number of books also published by the Trust.

ISBN 0 85151 502 9
144pp., paperback

Write for free 40pp illustrated Catalogue to:
THE BANNER OF TRUTH TRUST
3 Murrayfield Road, Edinburgh EH12 6EL
P.O. Box 621, Carlisle, Pennsylvania, 17013, U.S.A.